UNDERSTANDING
and
ANSWERING ISLAM

April 2017,
Melbourne, Australia

Edited by
Ruth J Nicholls

Arthur Jeffery Centre for the Study of Islam
Melbourne School of Theology
An affiliated college of the Australian College of Theology

mst press
Melbourne School of Theology

i

Understanding and Answering Islam, April 2017, Melbourne, Australia

Editor

Ruth Nicholls

Assistant Editor

Richard Shumack

Production and Cover Design

Ho-yuin Chan

Publishing Services

Published by MST Press
Thank you to Richard Shumack for his publishing services.

Arthur Jeffery Centre for the Study of Islam
Melbourne School of Theology
5 Burwood Highway, Wantirna, Victoria, 3152, Australia.
PO Box 6257, Vermont South, Victoria, 3133, Australia
Ph: +61 3 9881 7800, Fax: +61 3 9800 0121
info@JefferyCentre.mst.edu.au, www.mst.edu.au/

RZIM
RAVI ZACHARIAS INTERNATIONAL MINISTRIES

Ravi Zacharias
International Ministries

The primary mission of Ravi Zacharias International Ministries is to reach and challenge those who shape the ideas of a culture with the credibility of the Gospel of Jesus Christ. Distinctive in its strong evangelistic and apologetic foundation, the ministry of RZIM is intended to touch both the heart and the intellect of the thinkers and influencers of society through the support of the visionary leadership of Ravi Zacharias.

RZIM seeks to impact the heart and intellect of society's thinkers and influencers through:

• *Evangelism: RZIM shares the gospel through its global team of over 80 speakers and experts as well as its radio and television programs, podcasts, and publications that reach listeners and readers around the world.*

• *Apologetics: A team of evangelists and trained RZIM speakers participate in open forums, speaking engagements, panels, and debates to answer objections to Christianity with gentleness and respect.*

• *Spiritual Disciplines: RZIM strives to model and build Christ-like character through our books, group studies, and biblical resources.*

• *Training: RZIM hosts a range of programs and courses in the USA, UK, India, Singapore, and online, which are designed to instruct and equip all who desire to effectively contend for the Christian worldview.*

• *Humanitarian Support: RZIM's humanitarian arm, Wellspring International, identifies and financially equips existing organizations aiding women and children at risk and provides individual scholarships to support education, healthcare, and basic living needs.*

RZIM hosts several specific training initiatives including the Understanding and Answering Islam conference which brings together cutting-edge theory and practice in pursuit of understanding Islam and loving Muslims with the grace of Christ.

For further inquiries, please contact Dan Paterson at Dan.Paterson@rzim.asia

.

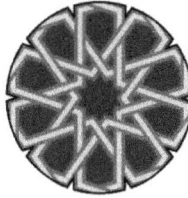

ARTHUR JEFFERY CENTRE FOR THE STUDY OF ISLAM,
Melbourne School of Theology, Australia

Formerly known as the Centre for the Study of Islam and Other Faiths it was renamed the Arthur Jeffery Centre for the Study of Islam in 2016. Arthur Jeffery was an Australian Methodist missionary who first went to India and ultimately developed proficiency in 19 languages. A contemporary of Samuel Zwemer, Jeffery became a recognized scholar of Islam who was invited to join the staff of the American University in Cairo. His book, "The Foreign Vocabulary of the Qur'an" which was first printed in 1938, still stands as the standard text in the field.

The Arthur Jeffery Centre for the Study of Islam is the only such Centre in Australia. Through its team of expert scholars and teachers of Islam it provides a variety of resources at both academic and public levels for those involved in or desiring to be involved in loving and meaningful engagement with Muslims.

The Centre is responsible for designing, preparing and teaching subjects approved by the Australian College of Theology at undergraduate and postgraduate levels relating to Islam. The Centre also aims for academic excellence through its publications which include not only scholarly works but also information for those who desire to increase their understanding of Islam. As part of its public engagement the Centre also holds open seminars and events, often joining with others sharing a similar vision and ethos. Staff are also available to speak at public programs.

In 2018 the Centre celebrates 10 years of operation and has established itself as a major centre for postgraduate studies in Islam.

For further information about the Centre and its activities, as well as opportunities to study Islam in a Christian context at both undergraduate and postgraduate levels, email info@JefferyCentre.mst.edu.au

TABLE OF CONTENTS

Editorial

This volume comprises the papers from the Understanding and Answering Islam conference held at Melbourne School of Theology in 2017. It is our hope that they represent the best of a generous yet robust Christian scholarly approach to Islam. The reader will benefit from the latest in cutting–edge research concerning the textual history of the Qur'an and Muslim traditions. Nevertheless, as the conference title suggests, the aim of the gathering was not simply to describe and evaluate particular features of Islam, but also to suggest ways forward in Christian engagement with Muslims around such features. Much of this practical side was covered in interactive seminars during the conference, however this relational goal is signalled by the fact that the more technical papers forming the bulk of this book are actually and theologically bookended by calls to deeply know and love Muslims.

Richard Shumack sets the tone with a description of the Muslim mindset, with special reference to the degree to which, and the reasons why, Muslims hold their religious beliefs to be true. This leads into a discussion of the sort of zeal that is appropriate for Muslims and Christians to hold and how that should impact upon Muslim-Christian relations. The volume then shifts gear as Andy Bannister examines a range of text-critical issues concerning the Qur'an. Starting with contemporary scholars' observations that (contra to popular Muslim conception) we really know very little of the Qur'an's textual origins, Bannister explores orality in the quranic text via examination of the Biblicist Adam and Iblis story contained in various *suras*. He concludes that the Qur'an does not exhibit Biblical copying so much as witness a retelling of Biblicist stories that were commonly spread throughout Arab oral culture.

Much traditional Muslim belief and practice is drawn not from the Qur'an, but from the Hadith. Bernie Power describes the history of how the Hadith collections came into being before identifying critical issues for Muslims raised in the Hadith. He

1

identifies external concerns, including serious questions of historical reliability, and internal problems involving both theological inconsistency and moral compromise in, for example, the treatment of women. This poses a dilemma for Muslims wanting to trust the Hadith, as well as an opportunity for apologetic engagement for Christians. Mark Durie covers similar ground with respect to the Qur'an. He argues that, unbeknown to most Muslims, the text of the Qur'an exhibits and describes a range of features that fail to accord with the traditional story of the origins of Islam. So, in Mark's words: "The geography does not fit. The variety of Arabic does not fit. The physical environment does not fit. The manuscript dating does not fit." This paper describes just how this is the case, and what implications that has for the traditional account of Islam.

A different approach to the quranic text is found in Peter Riddell's discussion of how Muslims throughout history have interpreted the opening chapter of the Qur'an — *Sura al-Fatiha*. This paper offers a concise introduction to the traditional principles of quranic interpretation, as well as opening the door to a thorny question for Muslim-Christian relations. There is a strong tradition of reading this chapter as speaking negatively about Jews and Christians. Given that the recitation of *al-Fatiha* forms a crucial part of daily Muslim devotion, how should Christians approach this? Peter concludes with suggestions.

Dan Paterson drew the conference, and draws this volume, to a close with an impassioned call for Christians to love Muslims enough to put the hard work into understanding Islam and then preparing for bold discussions, informed by studies in apologetics with Muslim friends and neighbours. This is something that all the contributors to the conference heartily endorse.

Richard Shumack
Director Arthur Jeffery Centre for the Study of Islam
Melbourne School of Theology
Academic Director, RZIM Understanding and Answering Islam

THE MUSLIM MINDSET

Richard Shumack

Approaches to Christian engagement with Muslims should be fundamentally shaped not by things like media exaggerations or personal experience/imagination but by a Biblical stance on the Muslim religious mindset. Unsurprisingly, the Scriptures approach this missional question with nuance and a deep appreciation of the nature of human spirituality. A short passage exploring important ideas around this is Romans 10:1–4. In this chapter Paul is referring to Jewish belief, but his ideas could equally be applied to traditional Muslim belief. The key dynamic Paul explores here is the interaction between zeal and righteousness; that is, between believing passionately and believing truly.

Romans 10:1-4 (NIVUK)[1]

> Brothers and sisters, my heart's desire and prayer to God for the Israelites is that they may be saved. [2]For I can testify about them that they are zealous for God, but their zeal is not based on knowledge. [3]Since they did not know the righteousness of God and sought to establish their own, they did not submit to God's righteousness. [4]Christ is the culmination of the law so that there may be righteousness for everyone who believes.

Muslim Zeal for Righteousness: Romans10:2–3

It soon becomes obvious to any who have engaged with Islamic communities that, like first century Jews, many Muslims are both passionate about their faith and extremely confident that their beliefs are true. It is important to understand the traditional

---

[1] New International Version - UK (NIVUK)
Holy Bible, New International Version® Anglicized, NIV® Copyright © 1979, 1984, 2011 by Biblica, Inc.® Used by permission. All rights reserved worldwide.
All subsequent Bible references have been sourced from this edition.

Islamic belief framework (or epistemology) that (supposedly) undergirds this confidence.[2]

First, Islam teaches that religion is properly **rational**. The idea here is that all religious beliefs should be sensible, clear and without contradiction. Second, Islam claims that religious beliefs must be **certain**. In Islam doubt is viewed negatively in the sense that doubting or questioning one's beliefs leads away from faith, and not towards it. Happily, for Muslims, Islam claims to offer that degree of certainty. Muslim philosopher Ismail al Faruqi makes the very strong claim that:

> *Unlike the faith of Christians, the imân (faith) of Islam is truth given to the mind, not to man's credulity. The truths, or prepositions, of imân are not mysteries, stumbling blocks, unknowable and unreasonable but critical and rational. They have been subjected to doubt and emerged from the testing confirmed and established as true. No more pleading on their behalf is necessary. Whoever acknowledges them as true is reasonable; whoever persists in denying or doubting is unreasonable. (Islam) ... comes to us armed with logical and coherent arguments and expects our acquiescence on rational, and hence necessary grounds...*[3]

Clearly, being told, and believing, that Islam is necessarily true leads to a very great felt confidence — even if this isn't the case.

Third, classical Islamic religion views righteousness primarily as **legal righteousness**. To be both right before God, and to live a righteous life is to fulfil all God's commands as they are revealed in the Qur'an and the Sunna (the words and example of Muhammad). It is important to recognise that just because Islam centres on law, that need not make it legalistic. Many Muslims will enjoy keeping the Sharia from their heart — not just because they are ordered to. Nevertheless, it is true that the traditional Islamic conception of the divine-human relationship is viewed essentially

---

[2]As this is a popular, rather than academic paper, I have avoided the use of detailed footnotes other than in direct quotes. Those wishing to view the detailed argument and references behind this paper should see Richard Shumack, R., *The Wisdom of Islam and the Foolishness of Christianity*, Island View Publishing: Sydney, 2014.

[3]Ismail Al-Faruqi, *Towards an Islamic Theory of Meta-Religion*, Part 1. Online: http://islamicstudies.islammessage.com/ResearchPaper.aspx?aid=572 cited1 April, 2017

in legislative terms, not personal. In Islam, Allah is a distant king, not an intimately involved Father.

This logically leads to a fourth idea: that good religious laws can properly be *enforced* on society. The logic here is simple and sensible. If the laws of Islam are good and truly divine, then it is best for all people that these laws form the legislative basis upon which society is built. As Seyyed Hossein Nasr puts it:

> Technically speaking, the Islamic ideal is that of a nomocracy, that is, the rule of Divine Law. It is true that all power, including political power belongs ultimately to God ... in the case of Islam, the rule of God ... is associated with that of the Shari'ah.[4]

It is easy to see how this sort of belief leads to the sort of extreme enforcement of the Sharia seen in the actions of groups like the Taliban and ISIS. For most Muslims, these forms of enforcement are extreme. Instead, they argue that Muslim laws can be enforced with compassion and within proper political systems. Perhaps they can. In any case, the whole idea of a nomocracy implies that Islam is *inherently* universal, political and enforceable.

Finally, and importantly, traditional Islam teaches that proper religion is *successful*. The understanding of success here is wide. It incorporates the building of a successful society and so Muslims are told in the Qur'an that they are the best of all people (Q3:110). But more importantly it involves humans being religiously successful before God. That is, Islam teaches Muslims that it is within their natural, unaided capacity to obey the divine law successfully enough to stand proudly before God on the last day pointing at their good works as meriting His gracious favour.

It is easy to see how, in combination, these fundamental beliefs can lead to an extraordinary zeal. If someone thinks their religious beliefs are *sensible, achievable, universal, enforceable* and on top of that *unquestionable* and *necessarily true*, that is a recipe for extreme conviction. It is also easy to see how Muslims can undermine Christian confidence with these zealous claims.

However, Christians need not be intimidated by any of these Muslim claims. The Muslim mindset is not simply a recipe

---

[4] S.H. Nasr, *The Heart of Islam*, HarperOne, San Francisco, 2004, pp. 148–150.

for zeal; it is a recipe for *misplaced* zeal since it eliminates any impetus toward carefully examining the truth of one's beliefs. As it happens this is a tragedy for Muslims, since none of these beliefs stand up to close scrutiny.

First, Islamic doctrine is *not at all obviously rational*. Take, for example, the most fundamental of Muslim doctrines: *tawhid* – or divine unity. Islam teaches an extreme version of divine simplicity in which God is allowed no complexity or division whatever. This is held with great pride as being obvious – in contrast to the incoherence of the notion of Trinity. Even a superficial reading of the philosophy of religion around this idea will reveal that it is not at all clear that the Muslim take on divine simplicity is coherent. The idea is greatly challenged. However, if we want to avoid deep philosophical thinking about this, there is a much simpler problem for Islam around *tawhid*. Traditional Islam also teaches that the Qur'an is an eternal book. But here's the problem: if the Qur'an is eternal, and God is eternal, and God is simply one, then how can the Qur'an be eternal? This is one of many similar problems where something superficially simple is, on reflection, very complicated.

Second, even if Muslim beliefs can be shown to be sensible, they are in *no way necessarily true and absolutely certain*. There are multiple reasons for this including: that the textual evidence shows Muslim claims around the reliability of the Qur'an are false; that the historical records about Muhammad's life are notoriously unreliable; and that there is no way of claiming that any limited human understanding of the eternal, infinite God eliminates any mysteries or unknowns. However, what's most ironic about al Faruqi's appeal to certainty is his claim that the core beliefs of Islam have been properly subjected to rigorous historical and philosophical' examination. This is simply untrue. Tricky philosophical questioning was largely shut down by Muslim religious authorities a millennium ago and even today there are practically no philosophy departments in Muslim universities. Moreover, beliefs to do with the supposedly pristine textual history of the Qur'an have *never* been carefully examined in the history of Islam. It is only in the last few decades that the Qur'an has been subjected to detailed textual analysis. This analysis is revealing texts riddled with intentional changes and a text development that cannot be squared with the traditional account. Clearly, core beliefs

6

to do with the Qur'an and Sunna are very far from being certain: and indeed, many are patently untrue. Sadly, though, Muslims have left this unexamined and so are in the dangerous epistemic position of feeling extraordinarily certain about beliefs that are desperately uncertain.

Third, it is unclear to me that all the laws of Islam show the proper signs of being divine, or even good. In my experience of living among Muslims, the Sharia when followed closely *appears oppressive* rather than life–giving. Here's one example "from below" (i.e. in the lives of ordinary Muslims). The Sharia teaches that fasting in Ramadan is obligatory, but that you do not need to fast if you are breastfeeding or pregnant. Nevertheless, if you skip the fast, you need to make it up at some stage in the future. I knew women who had been either breastfeeding or pregnant for around 12 years straight, and so had more than a year's worth of straight fasting to catch up on. All of them found this unreasonable and oppressive. Is this sort of demand really the sign of a loving and most gracious God? Not to my mind.

The problem becomes clear when examined "from above" too. If the Sharia really does produce the best of people, then why is the *track record of Muslim nations* so dire when it comes to matters of human flourishing? Countries that seek to enforce Islam on their population overwhelmingly rank poorly on most measures of human rights, particularly in their treatment of the weak and vulnerable. Muslim apologists might respond that this is due to these countries not taking their Islam seriously enough. But that simply raises the question why, if Islam is all it's cracked up to be in terms of success, can't it be successfully adopted by any nation? To my mind, the track record of the enforcement of Islam should lessen the zeal of Muslims.

Paul captures all this when he suggests that the sort of religion represented by Judaism and Islam displays a zeal that fails to be grounded in true knowledge:

> *For I can testify about them that they are zealous for God, but their zeal is not based on knowledge. ³ Since they did not know the righteousness of God and sought to establish their own, they did not submit to God's righteousness.* (Romans 10:2–3)

7

Islam bears all the hallmarks of a religion that hungers after righteousness but lacks the true knowledge of God's righteousness that can lead to a truly transformative life. This becomes all the more pointed when it comes to the person of Jesus.

True Righteousness: Romans 10:3

When Paul speaks of the righteousness of God he means the righteousness found in Jesus. The central message of the gospel of Christ is that his righteous sacrifice secures righteousness for humanity – both in terms of being right with God and living right lives. It is precisely this Christ-focused righteousness that Islam knows nothing about.

Of course, traditional Islam claims to embrace truth about Jesus. It recognises Jesus as the Messiah and teaches a range of things to do with his miracle working, his virgin birth, and his prophetic role. It is this that leads to the common Muslim notion that they hold Jesus in very high regard. I recall meeting a young Muslim friend who was wearing a t-shirt with "I Love Jesus" emblazoned across the front. On the back, it also said: "because I am a Muslim, and he was too!" I asked him just what it was about Jesus that he loved. Which of Jesus' actions? Which words? He smiled and confessed that it was merely a free t-shirt from the mosque and that he knew very little about Jesus' life. This amusing story is instructive: most Muslims, in fact, know very little of the historical Jesus and next to nothing about what it meant for him to be the Messiah.

However, the problem here is not simply ignorance of the Biblical Jesus. What is most telling is not what Islam affirms or ignores about Jesus, but what it denies. Later in Romans 10 Paul gets to the nub of how to secure righteousness, proclaiming that:

> ... *if you declare with your mouth, 'Jesus is Lord,' and believe in your heart that God raised him from the dead, you will be saved.* ...
> (Romans 10:9)

The core truths about Jesus that pertain to humans achieving righteousness are his divine lordship and his atoning death and resurrection. These are the two truths about Jesus that enable his fulfilment of the role of Messiah and ironically these are precisely the two truths Islam denies. What this means is that while Muslims are happy to accept a wide range of truths to do with Jesus,

8

they remain steadfastly "... ignorant of the righteousness of God" for salvation.

The upshot of all this is that many ordinary traditional Muslims are left in a philosophically dangerous mindset. For while they hold their religious beliefs with extreme confidence, they are reluctant to question or doubt their beliefs, and show a basic ignorance of a subject thought to be familiar – Jesus.

Christian Zeal: Romans10:1

Understanding the traditional Islamic religious mindset, and its teaching to do with Jesus, helps Christians recognise a range of epistemological barriers that need to be overcome in sharing the gospel with Muslims. For Muslims to accept Christian claims about Jesus will require them to make a massive shift in mindset. This sort of shift is difficult for all of us. It is a huge thing to be faced with the realization that your passions are not lined up properly with reality. Sometimes this is merely disappointing. For example, I have to deal with this in golf all the time. My true abilities are nothing like my felt confidence, so I always try to play unachievable shots. When it comes to religion though, a fundamental mindset shift is scary since it involves a deep core belief. For any Muslim to make this sort of epistemological shift they will need to fundamentally question things they have historically taken to be unquestionable. They will need to embrace a humbling recognition that perhaps Islam isn't the best of religions or Muslims the best of people. They may need to do some very hard and unfamiliar thinking about the true rationality of Islamic doctrine.

The challenge for Christian mission amongst Muslims is finding the appropriate sort of approach to trigger just this sort of existential wrestling in the Muslim mind. Here, obviously, apologetic arguments have their place. There is a right place to offer merely intellectual challenges to why others believe what they do and whether their beliefs are truly warranted. In the case of Muslim belief, their closed epistemology with its resistance to questioning often resists argument.

In addition to an intellectual discussion, Christians need to dent Muslims' supreme confidence that they hold absolute truth by displaying the sort of godly and spirit-filled life over time that leads to the possibility that a Muslim might recognise them as an epistemic authority on religion. For example, an encounter with a spirit-filled and grace-living Christian community might lead a Muslim to naturally question whether Islam really did produce the "best of all people", or whether they have been told the truth about Christianity and Islam. Similarly, any Muslim witnessing God answering the prayers of Christians will have no choice but to be confronted with the possibility that their beliefs about who God listens to are incorrect. In these and so many areas it is key to realise that when confronted with a zealous and largely closed mindset it is important not to merely tell people they are ignorant of truth, but to show them in ways that will strongly impact their felt confidence.

Of course, this model of engagement requires deep and long-term commitment by Christians to building substantial relationships with Muslims. The attitude of our hearts here is far more important than the adoption of correct ministry models. Again, Paul's discussion in Romans is helpful. Throughout the book of Romans he displays just the sort of missional heart that is required in reaching out to those who are naturally resistant to recognising Jesus as Lord. Indeed, the passage we have been focusing on comes in the middle of Chapters 9–11, a section which begins with the lament:

> *I speak the truth in Christ – I am not lying, my conscience confirms it through the Holy Spirit –* [2] *I have great sorrow and unceasing anguish in my heart.* [3] *For I could wish that I myself were cursed and cut off from Christ for the sake of my people, those of my own race ....* (Romans 9:1–3)

Crucially, Paul's missiological discussion is undergirded and framed by his love for his people. His deep longing for his neighbours to discover God's true righteousness is repeated in our passage:

> *Brothers and sisters, my heart's desire and prayer to God for the Israelites is that they may be saved ...* (Romans 10:1)

Paul's example reminds us that the best response to Muslim religious zeal is Christian zeal! This is partly because Christian zeal for the truth about Jesus is grounded in a long history of humble and rich examination of the reasons for our confidence. That is, Christian confidence that we believe the truth better corresponds to the evidence than Islam. More importantly, though, proper Christian zeal is necessary for it should lead not to unquestioning pride in being right, but to unwavering perseverance in loving

Muslims deeply and sharing our lives with them. The degree to which we exhibit this sort of zeal is the degree to which our love will show Muslims that Jesus is real (John 13:35).

WHERE DID THE QUR'AN COME FROM?

Andrew G. Bannister

Introduction

For over a thousand years, the methodology of Islamic scholarship has largely been to cite the opinions of previous generations rather than to actually ask the tough questions. Today, it is really only in the West — and even there, it is becoming rarer — that the Qur'an is subjected to rigorous scholarship. And so there is much that critical scholarship simply does not know about the Qur'an. Fred Donner of the University of Chicago writes:

> *Qur'anic studies, as a field of academic research, appears today to be in a state of disarray. Those of us who study Islam's origins have to admit collectively that we simply do not know some very basic things about the Qur'an – things so basic that the knowledge of them is usually taken for granted by scholars dealing with other texts.*[1]

What kind of "basic things" does Donner have in mind? He lists some examples:[2]

- How, where and when the Qur'an first originated
- Who were the first audience?
- How was it transmitted?
- Who first made the decision to codify it into written form?

The Quranic use of Biblicist Tradition

Another fascinating question concerns the Qur'an's use of "Biblicist" tradition: quranic material that has its roots in the Bible, the Jewish Talmud, or Christian apocryphal traditions. By some

---

[1] Fred M. Donner, 'The Qur'ān in Recent Scholarship: Challenges and Desiderata' in Gabriel Said Reynolds, ed., *The Qur'ān in Its Historical Context* (London: Routledge, 2008) 29-50, citing 29.

[2] See above

estimates, about 25% of the Qur'an is taken up with this kind of material.[3] Biblicist stories are found across the Qur'an and range in length from just a few verses to whole chapters — such as *Sura* 12 and its chapter-length treatment of the story of Joseph. The Qur'an assumes that its readers have heard the stories before and are familiar with them.

Let me give you an example of one such Biblicist story from the Qur'an — in some ways, the example *par excellence*, as it occurs seven times in the Qur'an:

> *Then we said to the angels: 'Bow down to Adam!'*
> *So they bowed—except Iblis. He was not amongst those who prostrated.*
> *(Allah) said: 'What prevented you from bowing when I commanded you?' Iblis replied: 'I am greater than he! You created me from fire and you created him from clay.'*
> *(Allah) said: 'Get down from here! It is not for you to show pride in here—get out! Verily you are among the most degraded.'*
> *(Iblis) said: 'Grant me respite until the Day of Resurrection.'*
> *(Allah) said: 'Verily you shall be among those who have respite.'*
> *(Iblis) said: 'Since you sent me astray, I shall lie in wait for them on the straight path!*
> *'Then I shall come upon them from in front and behind, from their right and their left. You shall not find most of them grateful or thankful.'*
> *(Allah) said: 'Get down from here, disgraced and rejected! Whoever follows you—truly I shall fill hell with you and them together!'*[4]

The Iblis and Adam story has an ancient history, predating the Qur'an by centuries. The oldest version we know is a Jewish version of the tale, found in the *Life of Adam and Eve* and dating to about 100BC. Other Jewish apocryphal books allude to the tale and the rabbinic literature makes frequent use of the story. Christian versions of the tale also exist, for example in the Syriac *Book of the*

---

[3] See e.g. Claude Gilliot, 'Narratives' in Jane Dammen McAuliffe, ed., Encyclopaedia of the Qur'an, Vol. 3 (Leiden: Brill, 2003) 516-527; Roberto Tottoli, 'Narrative Literature' in Andrew Rippin, ed., The Blackwell Companion to the Qur'an (Oxford: Blackwell, 2006) 467-480. See Reuven Firestone, Journeys in Holy Lands (Albany, NY: State University of New York Press, 1990) 6-21 for a discussion of how Biblicist material spread in the oral world of pre-Islamic Arabia.

[4] Q. 7:11-18. Parallel versions can be found in Q. 2:34; 15:29-43; 17:61-64; 18:50; 20:116-117; 38:71-83.

Cave of Treasures, which dates to the fourth century AD. It is thus very clear that the Iblis and Adam tale was very well-known in the centuries before Islam, circulating widely among both Jews and Christians — communities of whom were present in the Arabian Peninsula before Islam.

There are some interesting features, however, in the way the Iblis and Adam story is used in the Qur'an. In particular, the seven tellings of the story in the Qur'an differ in length — ranging from just a single verse (Q.18:50) to seventeen verses (Q.15:28–44). In each case, however, the basic story is the same:

- Each telling begins with a command to the angels to bow
- In each case the angels bow, but Iblis refuses
- Six of the seven tellings end the same way, with a warning of hell for Iblis and his followers

A fascinating question emerges: how do we explain not just the presence of so much Biblicist material in the Qur'an, stories like Iblis and Adam, as well as canonical stories like Joseph, Jonah and the fish, or Abraham and the sacrifice of his son — but how do we explain the *form* of those stories — multiple versions, different lengths, often highly allusive? What is going on?

Did the Qur'an "Borrow" or "Copy" these Stories?

One way to explain why so much Biblicist material exists in the Qur'an is to accuse Muhammad of copying. Muhammad was simply unoriginal goes the argument and borrowed heavily whatever he could lay his hands on.

Many Western scholars, especially in the late eighteenth through to the early twentieth century, popularised this kind of idea. A famous example of this approach is William St. Clair-Tisdall whose 1901 work, *The Sources of Islam*, attempted to extensively trace the many different sources, including both Jewish and Christian, upon which Muhammad had drawn in delivering the Qur'an.[5] St. Clair-Tisdall set out to trace Muhammad's sources and claimed to be able to directly identify many of them. He concluded:

---

[5] William St. Clair-Tisdall, 'The Sources of Islam' in Ibn Warraq, ed., *The Origins of the Koran* (New York: Prometheus Books, 1998 [1901]) 227-291, citing .

15

From all that has now been said, it must be clear to the reader that the Jewish writings, and specially the fanciful tales of the Talmud, formed one of the chief sources of Islam.[6]

Modern versions of the "borrowing thesis" exist: for example, in the 1970s, John Wansbrough in his hugely influential book *Quranic Studies*, argued that the Qur'an was the result of a long period of drawing from and reflecting on Biblicist material — not by one man (e.g. Muhammad) but by many people, over two centuries or more. He wrote:

> *[The Qur'an is] not the carefully executed project of one or many men, but rather the product of an organic development from originally independent traditions during a long period of transmission.*[7]

More recently, scholars like Christoph Luxenberg and Günter Lüling have argued that the material in the Qur'an made its way into Arabic from Syriac and Aramaic and was originally actually Christian in origin.[8] Again, the basic idea is that Muhammad and Islam *borrowed* much of what is the Qur'an from Christianity and Judaism.

There are, however, many problems with the "borrowing" thesis, which means that we need to be very careful about using it as an apologetic or polemic to deconstruct Muslim beliefs about the Qur'an. Let me point out three such problems:

First, there is the problem that there is almost no textual overlap between the Qur'an and the earlier alleged sources. Let me illustrate what I mean with a contemporary example. A few years ago, I was marking a PhD thesis when I became a bit suspicious about some of what the student had written. When I googled several significant sentences here was a classic case of plagiarism — the student had lifted 400 words – word for word – from Wikipedia.

---

[6] ibid., 257.

[7] John Wansbrough, *Quranic Studies* (New York: Prometheus, 2004 [1977]) 47.

[8] Christoph Luxenberg, *The Syro-Aramaic Reading of the Koran: A Contribution to the Decoding of the Language of the Koran* (New York: Prometheus, 2009) and Günter Lüling, *A Challenge to Islam for Reformation* (Delhi: Motilal Banarsidass, 2003). Angelika Neuwirth, 'Structure and the Emergence of Community' in Andrew Rippin, ed., *The Blackwell Companion to the Qur'an* (Oxford: Blackwell, 2006) 140-158, citing 140-158 suggests many quranic *suras* were originally liturgies, heavily influenced by Christian liturgical uses of scripture.

16

When you look at the Qur'an, however, and compare its tellings of Biblicist stories with the same stories in earlier writings, no such word for word overlap exists. Clearly, it's the same story being told, but direct copying fails to explain what is taking place.

A second problem for the "borrowing thesis" is that if Muhammad simply copied his Biblicist stories from earlier written sources, why does each telling in the Qur'an vary so widely? The Iblis and Adam story is told seven times and it varies considerably each time. Not only is each version different from the earlier Jewish and Christian stories, each is also different from the other six versions in the Qur'an. This is not what you'd expect if Muhammad had a copy of *The Book of the Cave of Treasures* open on his desk as he wrote.

Finally, a third problem is that the "borrowing thesis" requires written copies of these Jewish and Christian works to have been circulating, in writing, in Arabic at the time of Muhammad in order for him to have access to them to copy from. And there is little or no evidence that was the case.

Of course, Muslim scholars reject any hint, any suggestion that Muhammad *borrowed* from previous writings — they often appeal to the idea, the tradition, that Muhammad was illiterate. The early biographers of Muhammad make this claim, often rooting it in Q7:157:

> *Those who follow the messenger, the Prophet who can neither read nor write …*

Muslims often turn the claim that Muhammad was illiterate into an apologetic. I have lost count of how many Muslims over the years have said to me things along the lines of "How could an illiterate man produce a work like the Qur'an? It must be a miracle!"

The Qur'an and Oral Tradition

In fact, it was this very Muslim apologetic that first led to my interest in studying the Qur'an academically. You see there's a huge problem with that claim — not least that Muslim apologetics about Muhammad's illiteracy assumes that oral cultures were primitive, but this is not the case at all. For example, pre-Islamic Arabia was an oral culture and was famous for its extremely sophisticated poetry. Similarly, if we look at the period immediately *after*

Muhammad, we see that the Islamic tradition — history and biography and scriptural commentary — that began to develop and grow was also largely the work of oral preachers and storytellers.[9]

There is a whole field of scholarship — oral traditional studies — devoted to studying oral cultures. Its inception can largely be traced to two scholars — Milman Parry (1902–1935) and Albert Lord (1912–1991). Parry was a classicist, concerned with studying Homer's great poems, *The Iliad* and *The Odyssey*. Parry concluded that Homer was an oral poet, drawing upon traditions that pre-dated him and retelling it afresh for his audience. Homer's use of *highly formulaic language* was central to Parry's argument. Parry maintained that formulaic language was the key to the work of the oral poet or performer, allowing him to compose during the live performance, fluently in the traditional way. Rather than limiting this theory development to the study of inert texts, Parry searched for contemporary material that would enable him to undertake live field work. Working with his research assistant, Albert Lord, he found an active oral poetry tradition in Yugoslavia that enabled Parry to test and refine his theory of oral-formulaic composition.

Parry and Lord sought to discover how oral literature actually works by listening to, recording, and analysing oral poems performed by hundreds of singers. They concluded that for illiterate oral poets, each performance is unique.[10] Further, they maintained the use of *formulae*, or groups of words regularly deployed to express a key idea were crucial to live oral composition. They saw these formulae as similar to a repertoire of clichés and stock phrases[11], used time and again.

Parry and Lord came to the conclusion that the term "original" is largely meaningless in oral tradition, belonging instead to a literary paradigm. The "author" of an oral epic is the performer because the text is created "live" at the very moment of performance. The poet, singer, or storyteller draws upon a common

---

[9] See e.g. Jonathan P. Berkey, *Popular Preaching & Religious Authority in the Medieval Islamic Near East* (London: University of Washington Press, 2001).

[10] Albert B. Lord, *The Singer of Tales*, 2nd Ed. (Cambridge, MA: Harvard University Press, 2000) 8.

[11] ibid., 30.

pool or stock of traditional material familiar to his audience, but retells it afresh.

So, there are some key features of oral traditional material which include the use of formulaic language as well as conservative and fluid storytelling or creation.

Use of Formulaic Language
We live in a literary culture and so this idea is a little strange to us, but contemporary examples of formulaic language can still be found. For example, if a young child asks you to tell them the fairytale of Goldilocks and the Three Bears, you will probably commence your tale with the words "Once upon a time". You haven't *memorised* that formulaic phrase, you heard it from your parents, who heard it from their parents. It is simply a cultural artefact. Formulaic phrases can also be found in very modern forms of communication. Think of "text speak" — LOL, ROFL etc. Oral cultures, however, are full of hundreds, thousands of such formulaic phrases and indeed, the mark of an oral poet or storyteller's expertise is his ability to command them fluidly with ease. In his study of Homer's poems, for example, Parry found that about 25% of Homer is formulaic language — repeated phrases, ranging in length from a few words to a whole line.

Conservative and Fluid Telling
Another key hallmark of oral tradition is the idea that a tale or story is created afresh each time it is told. The basic story remains the same, but each telling is a fresh 'story'. Think again of my fairytale example: imagine a small child asks you to tell them the story of Goldilocks and the Three Bears. You comply, and we record it. The next day, they ask for the story again and you tell it again. We record this second telling. Now, imagine we were to transcribe these two recordings and compare them. Would they be word-for-word the same? No. The story would be the same — you'd have Goldilocks, and bears, and porridge and so forth — but the wording would show fluidity. You would have created what is called *a performance variant*. Two versions of the same story whose differences come from the fact it was performed, not memorised or recited.

Interestingly, both of these features of oral tradition — formulaic language and performance variants – are found in the Qur'an.

Applying this to the Qur'an

The seven versions of the Iblis and Adam story in the Qur'an each tell the same basic story, but show flexibility in the wording, and some versions are shorter or longer than others. What can explain that feature? That they are *performance variants* explains it remarkably well — they are multiple oral tellings of the same story, told on different occasions and in different settings. As Fred Donner puts it, such passages in the Qur'an are perhaps best explained as:

> *[T]ranscripts of different oral recitations of the same story made in close succession, something like different recordings of a politician's stump speech delivered numerous times over a few days or weeks.*[12]

What about the other indicator of oral tradition — formulaic language? Well, studying this was what I did in my PhD work, from 2004-2011, now published as *An Oral-Formulaic Study of the Qur'an*. Drawing on my background in computer science, I developed computer software that analysed the entire Arabic text of the Qur'an, by searching for formulaic phrases — short repeated phrases that occur time and time again. Computers have been used in biblical studies for many years but are only recently beginning to make inroads into Islamic studies. The computer analysis reveals a number of things:

- between 24% and 52% of the Qur'an is formulaic. That means that depending how you do the analysis (whether you look for longer or shorter formulaic phrases), up to half of the quranic text consists of formulaic language, a key indicator of oral tradition

- formulaic phraseology occurs throughout the Qur'an and is found in every chapter. It is occurs most frequently in the narrative sections, like the Iblis and Adam stories, which are extremely formulaic

---

[12] Donner, 'The Qur'ān in Recent Scholarship: Challenges and Desiderata', 34.

- some of the formulaic phrases revealed by computer analysis occur over 40 times and many are staples of quranic diction, including:

  - *kull + shay + qadīr* ("... power over all things ...") — 52 times
  - *lladhīna + āmanū + 'amilū* ("... those who believe and work ...") [often followed by a form of *ṣlḥ*, righteousness] — 50 times
  - *llāh + ghafūr + raḥīm* ("... Allah is most merciful ...") — 46 times
  - *fī + sabīl + llāh* ("... in the way of Allah ...") — 46 times

In short, the Qur'an looks like it has its roots in oral tradition — not written tradition, oral tradition. It shows all of the signs we would expect from material that was originally not just spoken out loud but constructed, extemporaneously, in oral performance. This explains why stories like Iblis and Adam — and indeed much of the Qur'an — looks the way it does, steeped in performance variants and formulaic language.

Conclusions

How does all of this help to explain the question we set out to examine — why the Qur'an contains so much Biblicist material — stories like the tale of Iblis and Adam, with their roots in Jewish and Christian tradition? We saw that "literary borrowing" doesn't work as an explanation. How might the fact that the Qur'an looks like an oral traditional product help us?

We need to remember how oral cultures work. Oral cultures often involve story swapping and trading, as Reuven Firestone wrote:

> *When people trade with one another in societies where the anonymous department store or shopping mall has not yet overtaken the institution of the private vendor of goods, merchants and customers engage in social intercourse that far transcends the simple transfer of merchandise. This kind of trade involves interaction in which traders swap stories and anecdotes as well as goods. At the annual Arabian trading fairs, where diverse tribal units from broad geographic areas gathered, as well as during other occasions of inter-communal*

interaction, biblical stories would naturally be traded with local Arabian religious tales.[13]

Oral cultures also produce works — when their tales and traditions are eventually written down — that have a number of features, including formulaic language and performance variants.

Formulaic Language

It is formulaic language that allows an oral poet, storyteller, or singer to construct his tale, song, or poem live, in front of an audience, without pausing for thought. He knows the right formula, just as you know "Once upon a time …" is the way to start a fairytale or your teenage son knows "LOL" is the right way to end a text message.

Performance Variants

An oral singer, poet, or storyteller does not remember each story word for word, but constructs it afresh in each performance.

Both of these features are found extensively throughout the Qur'an.

There are other clues, too. For example, we know that before the rise of Islam, the culture was oral and known for its oral poetry in particular. We know the period immediately after Muhammad's death, when Islamic tradition began to take shape, was oral. We have orality both before and after Muhammad. In archaeology, if you want to understand the find you have just dug up, it is important to consider its context — what lay on top of it, what lay under it. I suggest we need to do the same for the Qur'an — putting it back into the oral milieu from which it emerged to understand it.

Finally, there is the biographical literature about Muhammad which grew up in early Islam. It preserves the folk memory of Muhammad preaching extemporaneously; a situation would arise, a question would be asked and immediately, he would have a quranic verse or *sura* ready. That looks like the oral preacher, oral storyteller at work. *In short, the Qur'an looks like an oral traditional work.*

---

[13] Firestone, *Journeys,* , 6, cf. 15-18.

Why is this important? This is not just an answer to a scholarly question — this is, my friends, apologetic dynamite, for a number of reasons:

- First, it puts the Qur'an into its context and shows that the Qur'an did not drop miraculously from heaven, but has a context into which it fits perfectly. That is a very difficult fact for a Muslim to hear.

- Second, the Qur'an has human fingerprints all over it. They are very oral fingerprints, for sure, but they are very human fingerprints. Back in England, I love to walk the hills and mountains of northern England and often stumble across caves and tunnels in the hillside — remnants of mining, for lead, copper and iron, that date back to Roman times. How can you tell the really old tunnels from the more recent Victorian ones — by the pick marks in the rock walls. Tools leave their marks on what they have hewn and so it is with the Qur'an. Muhammad used the tools and techniques of the oral performer as he first preached the material that now forms the Qur'an — and those oral tools have left marks — performance variants, formulaic language — behind for us to find.

Islam stands on two pillars: the Qur'an and Muhammad. My work knocks out one of those pillars entirely.

One last thought: oral traditional approaches have been used on a number of different cultures and traditions, including the Bible, and we see several features of orality in places in the Gospels, especially in the parables. *This is exactly what we'd expect to find —* Jesus was an oral storyteller, an oral preacher, who told many of his parables probably hundreds of times in the villages and towns where he travelled and spoke. If we can find oral features in the gospels, it shows they are early — not the later literary inventions of the early church, as some sceptics like to claim. But for Islam, the presence of signs of orality in the Qur'an is devastating — it is supposed to be a written book, a copy of the eternal tablets that rest in heaven alongside Allah. It should not have oral fingerprints all over it.

Thus, we have a powerful tool — oral traditional studies — that may be applied to both the Qur'an and the Gospels. This tool simultaneously undermines the former, whilst building up the latter.

In conclusion, the best explanation for the Biblicist material in the Qur'an is not that Muhammad copied from previous written texts, but that he was an oral preacher, fishing from the common pool of religious stories—some Jewish, some Christian, some pagan — that were circulating around the Arabia of his day. His oral environment and his oral fingerprints, as it were, have left their mark on the Qur'an today. We can show it to be a very human product indeed.

PROBLEMS WITH THE HADITH

Bernie Power

Definition of Hadith

The word "*hadith*" means "saying". The hadith collections are basically the sayings and actions of Muhammad and his early companions. The hadith are nowadays generally restricted to those sayings and actions which are gathered in one of the many collections of the hadith.

Origin of the Hadith

When Muhammad died in 10 AH/632 AD,[1] he left behind about 100,000 followers. Some of them had known him all his life, but most of them were newcomers to Islam and the majority had never met him or seen him.

According to Islamic sources, the oral recitation of the Qur'an had been completed by this time due to Muhammad's death, and it would soon be collated and authorised. But the Qur'an suffered from serious deficiencies. One was its size. It was only 6,200 verses long, about three-quarters of the size of the New Testament. Because of this, it lacked a lot of important details about how to live the Muslim life. When Muhammad was alive, he could be asked for a revelation or advice, or people could observe what he did and try to imitate him. But now he was dead, and most Muslims did not know him or what he had done.

There was also the problem of new situations which Muhammad had never faced. What might he have done if he had

---

[1] In this paper, most dates will be given in the AH/AD format, indicating the Islamic Hijri calendar years, based on twelve lunar months beginning from the migration or *hijra* of the first Muslims to Medina/Yathrib in 622 AD, and the Gregorian solar calendar, with years designated as *anno domini* (AD) used throughout the world today.

faced these same issues? Some knowledge of what he had done would allow people to draw some analogies from which to make decisions. Consequently, there was a widespread curiosity about Muhammad among people who had never met him. So, stories about Muhammad began to circulate. These were all oral, because, according to some accounts, Muhammad forbade his followers from writing down anything he said apart from direct revelations from Allah which were recorded as part of the Qur'an. But there was another problem.

Islam quickly began to extend its reach. When Muhammad died, Islamic rule covered only the Arabian Peninsula. Under the early *caliphs* or leaders, Muslim armies began to invade and occupy the countries around them. Within 20 years, they had overrun all of the Levant, parts of North Africa up to modern Libya, and much of modern Iran and Iraq. Within 100 years, they had spread across the north of Africa across the Gibraltar Strait and occupied the Iberian Peninsula, encompassing Portugal and Spain, had pushed north into the Caucasus, and eastwards overrunning Afghanistan and Pakistan. Within this period, two-thirds of former Christendom had fallen under Islamic control. In this first 100 years, Muslim armies did not lose a single major battle. It was only at Poitiers in France, against Charles Martel in 732 AD that they first tasted a significant defeat. But the Islamic juggernaut rolled on, subjugating country after country.

The Collection of the Hadith
As Islam began to spread to other countries through military conquest, non-Arabs were forced to live under Muslim rule or embrace Islam, so curiosity about the founder of Islam spread to those who had never known him. Muhammad's companions were being killed in battle, or dying of old age, so it became imperative that the stories about him be preserved. So people began to write down the stories they had heard. However, it was not until a century after Muhammad died that the first written collection was compiled. The first seven compilations are reflected in Table 1. None of these were eyewitness accounts, and none of them were based on written records.

If we look at the timeline below, we see that Muhammad died in 632 AD at 63 years of age. His companion Abu Huraira died 50 years later. It is said that he was 79. He told stories about Muhammad to Ibn Munabbih who died 69 years later. If he had heard from Abu Huraira when he was 30 years old, he would have died at 90. These life-spans seem remarkable considering that average life expectancy during the early Caliphate period was estimated to be only 35 years.[2]

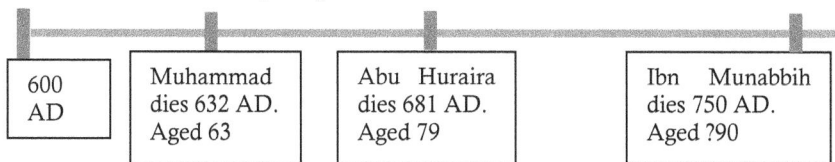

600 AD	Muhammad dies 632 AD. Aged 63	Abu Huraira dies 681 AD. Aged 79	Ibn Munabbih dies 750 AD. Aged ?90

Timeline 1: Muhammad's Companions

Some of these proto-collections did not include full *isnads* or chains of transmission for the Hadith they included, nor was there a classification for distinguishing between the genuine, the dubious and the forged. Consequently, these early compendia were considered to be less reliable than the later canonical collections. In the two hundred years after Muhammad's death, only about thirty collections of the hadith had been compiled. However, during the third century of Islam, over fifty new collections came into existence. This was the golden age of collections of the Hadith.

As these accounts of Muhammad's life and early Islamic history were gathered, it was found that discerning real traditions from fictitious accounts was no straightforward task.

> "*In the first two centuries after Muhammad's death the number of Hadiths increased in direct proportion to the demand. Whenever the community faced a new issue each party concerned would seek authority for its view in a Hadith. This became a flourishing industry.*"[3]

The common people had an insatiable appetite for stories about Muhammad, and hadith narrators were only too willing to oblige. One man, 'Abd al-Karim Abu 'l-Auja, confessed to fabricating 4,000 Hadiths. He was crucified c155/772 by Muhammad b

---

[2] http://www.sarahwoodbury.com/life-expectancy-muslim-world-verses-christian-world-in-the-middle-ages/ cited 5th May, 2018

[3] Hitti 1970:42

Table 2:

Collections of Hadith based on years after Mohammad's Death (YAM)

Compiler	Died	YAM	Some details of the collection
Hammam ibn Munabbih	750 AD	122	taught by Abu Huraira (d.61/**681**) 138 Hadith
Ibn Shibab al-Zuhri	741 AD	114	requested by the Caliph 'Umar II (d.101/**720**)
Ibn Jurayj	767 AD	140	called *Musannaf* "categories"
Ma`mar bin Rashid	770 AD	143	called *Musannaf* "categories"
Sufyan al-Thawri	778 AD	151	
Malik bin Anas	795 AD	169	called *Muwatta* 'smooth/easy layout'
Abd al-Razzaq al-San`ani	826 AD	201	called *Musannaf*

YAM – Years after the death of Muhammad.

Sulaiman b. 'Ali, governor of Basrah.[1]

By the beginning of the third century of Islam (200/815), there was a plethora of hadith narratives in circulation. Margoliouth claims that al-Bukhārī had heard 90,000 of them.[2] Guillaume quotes a figure of 600,000 but notes "[t]hese figures must be taken with a grain of salt."[3]

It was the classification of the hadith into *sahih* ("sound/authentic"), *hasan* ("good"), *da'if* ("weak") and *mawduu'* ("forged") by Ali ibn al-Madini (d. 234/848) that moved towards a solution.[4] His student Muhammad al-Bukhārī made the controversial decision to include only *sahih* hadith in his collection.

The development of higher standards of assessment led to greater confidence in the veracity of the accounts included in these *sahih* collections. Generally, it was the *isnads* which were assessed. Previous written records were not relied upon since only oral transmission was considered legitimate. By now, 200 to 250 years after Muhammad had died, each hadith had an oral transmission link back to the Prophet, requiring between 5 and 10 informants.

Tedious research was often accompanied by wide and perilous travel. Hadith collectors tried to ascertain whether each informant in every *isnad* was suitable for the task. They asked: were the transmitters known to be truthful and consistent? Were they of sufficient age to be reliable to pass the information on? Had they been in the same country at the same time as the person they had heard the hadith from? Every account and every narrator needed to be checked. The hadith collectors wanted to ensure that they were

---

[1] according to
http://www.usc.edu/dept/MSA/fundamentals/Hadithsunnah/scienceofHadith/asb7.html accessed on 17th April, 2008
[2] David Margoliouth *Mohammed* (London & Glasgow: Blackie and Son, 1939), p12
[3] Alfred Guillaume *The Traditions of Islam: An Introduction to the study of the Hadith Literature* (Beirut: Khayats, 1966), p28
[4] "Imaam Tirmidhi's Contribution – Chapter Four" (http://web.archive.org/web/20070626193607/http://www.jamiat.org.za/isinfo/tirmidhi04.html). Web.archive.org. Archived from the original (http://www.jamiat.org.za/isinfo/tirmidhi04.html) cited 1st October, 2017

gathering the most unadulterated and pertinent accounts of the life of their beloved Prophet and his companions.

Some accounts had multiple attestations, originating from a number of Companions of the Prophet, and conveyed by a variety of chains of transmission. They were called *mutawātir*. The existence of several different persons of the same generation agreeing on the saying or action of Muhammad or his Companions meant that it was more likely to be accurate. When Jalāluddīn al-Suyuti assessed the *sahih* traditions which complied with this standard, he came up with 113 hadiths. But he did set the standard high, requiring that each be attested by at least ten narrators at every link.[5] The vast majority of hadith were *ahad* ("isolated"), with fewer verifiers in each generation: they were divided into *mashhūr* ("famous") with more than two reporters, *'azīz* ("rare") with only two reporters, and *gharīb* ("strange") with a single reporter at some stage in the *isnad.*

It may have been these more rigorous methodologies that caused some collections to be accepted as authoritative and deemed as canonical. The first among these was by Muhammad b. Isma'il al-Bukhārī (d.256/870). He whittled the alleged 600,000 oral reports down to 2,602 reports which he accepted as authentic or *sahiah.* With repetitions of the same or similar accounts from different *isnads* it grew to 7,275. This was a significant reduction from Abu Bakr bin Abi Shaybah's list of 37,943 hadith of a few years earlier. Al-Bukhārī's student Muslim bin al-Hajjaj (d.261/875) completed the second *sahih* collection. Many of the narrations are the same as al-Bukhārī's, but Muslim's classification was more systematic. Four other compilations complete the so-called *al-kutub al-sitta* "the six books" which are considered the major canonical collections today. They are: the compilations of Abu Dawud (d.275/889), al-Nisa'ī (d.303/915), al-Tirmidhi (d.279/892), and ibn Majah (d.273/886). Of these "six books", the first "two approved" versions, the *sahihayn*, of al-Bukhārī and Muslim are seen as the pinnacle of reliability among the Sunni hadith. All of the "six books" collections are extant.

---

[5] http://islamicencyclopedia.org/public/index/topicDetail/id/744 cited 1st October, 2017

When first published, the "authentic" collections were challenged by the *ahl-al-hadīth* ("people of the Hadith"), who strongly promoted the use of the hadith. Their concern was that any writings which drew on hadiths not listed in these collections would be scoffed at by another group of Muslims, the *ahl-al-ra'y* ("people of the opinion"), who felt human reasoning was a key element in discerning Islamic teachings. Unlisted hadith could be easily dismissed with the charge: "That is not in the *Sahīh!*"

But a ready answer to this charge existed: the collectors admitted that they had been selective in their choices.

Under fire from such critics, al-Bukhāri and Muslim defended themselves by saying that their books did not include all the sahīh hadiths in circulation. Al-Bukhāri only selected sahīh traditions useful for his legal discussions, and Muslim had limited his book to hadiths whose authenticity he believed was agreed by all.[6]

Al-Hākim al-Naysābūrī (d.405/1014) in his *al-Mustadrak* compiled a list of 8,800 hadith which he considered *sahīh* but had been omitted from the *Sahīhayn*. In selecting the hadith, he tried to adhere as closely as possible to the strict rules which al-Bukhārī and Muslim applied. Both Abū al-Hasan al-Dāraqutnī (d.385/995) and Abū Dharr al-Harawī (d.430/1038) had earlier compiled one volume called *Ilzāmāt* ("Addendums") with similar lists.[7]

Clearly the "six collections" were not seen, in the early days at least, to be the only authorised lists of authentic Hadith. There were elements of these Hadith collections which were commendable in their honesty but may not have inspired confidence. Dozens of times al-Bukhārī's Hadith attest their own shortcomings, with narrators making statements such as: "I've forgotten", or "I'm not sure", or "he said something like." At other times, there are differences in what the narrators said. One may have disagreed with another narrator,[8] suggested an alternative,[9] or

---

[6] Brown, *Hadith*, p38

[7] Brown, *Hadith*, p42

[8] Al-Bukhārī 1:470; 3:386, 511, 683; 4:55, 410

[9] Al-Bukhārī 1:542; 3:358; 4:124; 5:191; 6:222, 235, 294; 8:164

added something.[10] At other times, doubt is cast on the entire account, with a statement like: "But this report is not confirmed by an authentic narration."[11]

The admission of these discrepancies has caused some scholars to cast doubt on the hadith accounts. At other times the editors were more forthcoming with their confessions. After listing four supplications of Muhammad, Sufyan added: "This narration contained three items only, but I added one. I do not know which one that was."[12] Although Muhammad listed forty deeds which could result in Paradise for those who performed them, one chronicler struggled to identify even fifteen of them.[13] Clearly there was much information which had been passed on by Muhammad at one time but was not lost to antiquity. The hadith that were compiled, even in those early days, were never comprehensive. Ibn Manda (d. 395/1004–5) contends that Abū Dāwūd included weak hadiths if he could find no reliable reports on a certain subject.[14] These factors left the field open for further collections.

Voll notes the shortcomings of these anthologies:

"These great collections are not, however, canonical. No institution has ever officially accepted them, and the verifying community has been the general consensus of the community, which is flexible. The six collections contain contradictory material, and Muslims, from time to time, go outside of the body of Hadiths contained in these collections for authoritative opinion."[15]

In fact, some scholars claim that the sixth collection should be the *Muwatta* of Malik b. Anas instead of the *Sunan* of Ibn Majah. Nor

---

[10] Al-Bukhārī 1:581; 2:516; 3:205; 6:224; 7:231

[11] Al-Bukhārī 3:779

[12] Al-Bukhārī 8:358

[13] Al-Bukhārī 3:800

[14] see Muhammad b. Ishaq Ibn Manda, *Shurū} al-a'imma/Risala fi bayan fadl al-akhbār wa sharh} madhāhib ahl al-athār wa haqīqat al-sunan wa tas}h}īh al-riwāyāt*, ed. 'Abd al-Rahmān b. 'Abd al-Jabbār al-Farāwā'ī (Riyadh: Dār al-Muslim, 1416/1995), p73 cited in Jonathon Brown, *The Canonization of al-Bukhārī and Muslim: The Formation and Function of the Sunni Hadith Canon* (Boston: Leiden, 2007),p55 fn.19

[15] John Obert Voll *Islam: Continuity and Change in the Modern World* (Essex: Longman, 1982), p24

were some scholars impressed with the limited size and topic range of the so-called "canonical" collections.

Within a few years of its publication, Muslim's collection alone attracted at least six "complementary" works by those convinced that he had omitted some significant hadith accounts. They include the collections of
- al-Fadl b. al-'Abbâs al-Sa'igh (d.270/883)
- Ibn Rajâ (d.286/894)
- Ahmad b. Salama al-Bazzâr (d.292/905)
- Abu Ja'far al-Hiri (d.311/923)
- Abu 'Awana (d.312/933)
- Abu'l-'Abbas al-Sarrâj (d.313/934)

There were also at least eight later collections which sought to include what was lacking in the combined works of al-Bukhārī and Muslim. They include two *mustadrak* ("supplement") works, by al-Hakim al-Nisaburi (d.405/1014), and Abu Dharr al-Harawi (d.430/1038).

At least six *mustakhraj* collections, which added fresh *isnads* to pre-existing accounts, were published. They included works by Ibn al-Akhram (d.344/955), al-Mâsarjisi (d.365/975), Abu Bakr al-Isma'ili (d.371/981), al-Ghitrifi (d.377/987), Abu Bakr al-Barqani (d.425/1033), and Abu Muhammad al-Khallâl (d.439/1047). Clearly these authors did not consider the *sahihayn* to be the final word on the hadith.

Shi'a collections of the Hadith
One of Muhammad's greatest mistakes was his failure to designate a clear successor or *Caliph*. Because he died with no male offspring, a dispute arose at his death about who should lead the Muslim *umma* or nation. Muhammad's best friend and one of his fathers-in-law, Abu Bakr, took the role. He was succeeded at his death by 'Umar bin Khattab, one of Muhammad's sons-in-law, who ruled for ten years (634-644 AD) until he was killed by a slave. He was replaced by another of Muhammad's fathers-in-law, Uthman bin Affan. By this time, the Islamic empire had expanded greatly, and Uthman put his relatives into positions of power where they oppressed others and became very wealthy. Uthman was killed by several other Muslims in 656 AD and replaced by Ali bin Abu Talib, Muhammad's cousin and also a son-in-law. However, by now the Muslims were divided into two groups: those who believed

that the first successor to Muhammad should have been Ali, called 'the party of Ali' or *Shiat Ali*, and those who accepted the first three caliphs because they followed the path or *sunna* of Muhammad. There were historical scores to settle, and so the battle-lines were set. Over time, the division between Sunni and Shi'a widened. Shi'a scholars refused to accept any hadith transmitted by Aisha, Muhammad's favourite wife, because of her opposition to Ali bin Abu Talib at the Battle of the Camel (36/656). Aisha was an important contributor to "the six books". Only Muhammad's son-in-law Ali and the early imams were counted as reliable by the Shi'a, so all of their hadith assemblages required one of them as a transmitter. Consequently, a series of Shi'a hadith collections were gathered. They include the works of:

- Abu Ja'far al-Kulayni (d.328/939) *Al-Kāfi fi 'ilm al-dīn* "Sufficiency in Religious Knowledge"
- Shaikh Ali al-Babuya al-Kummi (d.381/991) *Kitāb man-lā-yastahzirahu 'l-Faqīh* "Non-conjectural Book of Jurisprudence"
- Abū al-Qāsim 'Alī b. al-Muhassin al-Tanūkhī (d. 407/1016), *Sahīh collection*
- Shaikh Abu Ja'far al-Tūsi (d.460/1068) *Al-tahzīb* "Cultural Education" and *Al-istibsār* "Seeking Insight"
- Sayyid al-Rāzi (d.406/1015) *Najhu al-balāghah* "The Peak of Excellence"
- Muhammad Baqir al-Majlīsi (d.1110/1700) *Bihār al-anwār* "The Ocean of Lights", consisting of a massive 110 volumes.

New anthologies
Despite the existence of the canonical collections and the alternative voice of the Shi'a compendia, scholars continued to compile new anthologies. They included:

- The *Sahih* of Ibn Khuzaymah (d.311/923)
- *Al-Jāmi' al-sahīh* by Abū Hafs 'Umar b. Muhammad al-Bujayrī of Samarqand (d. 311/924)
- *Tahdhīb al-Āthār* ("Reformation of the Ancients") by Muhammad ibn Jarir al-Tabari (d.311/923).
- *Sunan* of Dāraqutnī (d.385/995)
- *Ṣahīh Ibn Ḥibbān* by Abu Hatim al-Tamimi al-Busti (d.354/965)

- *Al-Mustadrak alaa al-Sahihain* ("Supplement for What is Missing from al-Bukhārī and Muslim") by Hākim al-Nishaburi (d. 405/1012)
- *Talkhis* (lit. "abridgement") *al-Mustadrak* by al-Dhababī (d.749/1348)

As the new Gregorian millennium progressed, significant hadith works continued to be published. Often, they were reworkings of, or reactions to, previous collections. They included:
- *Masabih al-Sunnah* ("Lights of the Path") by Abu Muhammad al-Farra' al-Baghawi (d.516/1122)
- *Al-Mawdū'āt al-Kubrā* ("A Great Collection of Fabricated Traditions") by Abul-Faraj Ibn Al-Jawzi (d. 597/1200)
- *Riyadh as-Saaliheen* ("The Gardens of the Righteous") by Yahiya ibn Sharaf al-Nawawi (d.676/1278)
- *Mishkat al-Masabih,* ("The Niche of Lights") by Al-Tabrizi d. 741/1340)
- *al-Ihsan fi Taqrib Sahih Ibn Hibban* by Ali ibn Balban (d. 739/1339)
- *Majma' al-Zawa'id wa Manba' al-Fawa'id* ("Collection of the Additions") by Ali ibn Abu Bakr al-Haythami (d.807/1405)
- *Mawarid al-Zam'an ila Zawa'id Ibn Hibban* by Ali ibn Abu Bakr al-Haythami (d.807/1405)
- *Bulugh al-Maram min Adillat al-Ahkam* ("Attainment of the Objective According to Evidences of the Ordinances") by al-Hafidh ibn Hajar al-Asqalani (1372-1448).

Counting both Sunni and Shi'a collections, over one hundred collections of the hadith are known to have been compiled. Many others were written and have disappeared throughout history.

Content of the Hadith
In determining whether a particular account or 'hadith' should be accepted into a collection, it was not only the *isnad* which came under scrutiny. The *matn* or content of the hadith was also assessed. Al-Siba'i claims that fifteen criteria were used by the early hadith collectors to separate genuine accounts from forgeries.

> *Hadith reports must not conflict with fundamental principles of reason, general principles of wisdom and morality, facts known by*

direct observation, or fundamental principles of medicine. They must not contain absurd statements or statements contrary to the teaching of more authoritative sources as the Qur'an. They should coincide with historical conditions during the time of the Prophet, and reports of events that have been widely known should be rejected if only a single witness reports them. Finally, they should not encourage vice, contradict reason, or promise large rewards or grave punishments for insignificant acts.[16]

Those who oppose the hadith today claim that some accounts fall far short of these standards. We can apply these standards to some of the hadith in al-Bukhārī's and Muslim's collections to determine whether they fulfil the criteria.

Sahih al-Bukhārī states: "Satan stays in the upper part of the nose all night." (vol. 4 no. 516) In Sahih Muslim vol.1 no. 462, it is recorded that Abu Huraira reported that the Apostle of Allah said: "When any one of you awakes from sleep and performs ablution, he must clean his nose three times, for the devil spends the night in the interior of his nose." As a result of this hadith, Muslims perform nasal ablutions by sucking water into the nostrils three times and flushing the water out. These ablutions are performed first thing in the morning and also during the *wudu* or ritual washing before prayers. The commentary on this verse states:

we should believe that Satan actually stays in the upper part of one's nose, though we cannot perceive how, for this is related to the unseen world of which we know nothing except what Allah tells us through his Apostle Mohammed [sic]. (Muslim 1:462)

Although a recognition of spiritual beings which are not physically discerned is found in many religious belief systems, these hadith assume Satan's omnipresence, whereas many religious traditions would accept that this attribute belongs only to God himself.

According to Sahih al-Bukhārī 7:673 and 4:537, Muhammad said:

If a fly falls in the vessel of any of you, let him dip all of it (into the vessel) and then throw it away, for in one of its wings there is a disease

---

[16] Al-Siba'i al-Sunnah, pp.250, 251 cited in Mohsen Haredy Hadith Textual Criticism: A Reconsideration
http://www.onislam.net/english/shariah/contemporary-issues/islamic-themes/422169.html#27 1st October, 2017

and in the other there is healing (antidote for it) i.e. the treatment for that disease.

Modern science recognises that flies are responsible for the spread of many diseases through the transmission of microbes.

House flies are strongly suspected of transmitting at least 65 diseases to humans, including typhoid fever, dysentery, cholera, poliomyelitis, yaws, anthrax, tularemia, leprosy and tuberculosis. Flies regurgitate and excrete wherever they come to rest and thereby mechanically transmit disease organisms. [17]

Consequently, food and drink for human consumption should be protected from contact with flies as much as possible. Fly-contaminated food and drink should be discarded and areas affected by flies cleaned with antiseptic. The ingestion of food and drink which has been subject to contact with flies should not be encouraged.

In Sahih al-Bukhārī 7:448 and 7:447, 446 and 1:236, 237, Muhammad said: "If you find a dead mouse in a container of butter-fat, throw away the mouse and the portion of butter-fat around it, and eat the rest." The same rules of adulterated food described above apply.

According to al-Bukhārī 1:234 and 2:577 and 5:505 and 7:589, 590,

Some people of 'Ukl or 'Uraina tribe came to Medina and its climate did not suit them. So the Prophet ordered them to go to the herd of (Milch) camels and to drink their milk and urine (as a medicine).

Drinking camel's urine has not been shown to have any positive medicinal value, but it could lead to sickness and even death. The World Health Organisation issued a warning against MERS, or Middle East Respiratory Syndrome Coronavirus, which leads to fevers, breathing problems, pneumonia, kidney failure and other deadly complications. It can result from contact with camels and camel products. In 2014, 681 cases of the disease were identified in Saudi Arabia, leading to 204 deaths. [18]

---

[17] http://ento.psu.edu/extension/factsheets/house-flies cited 5 May, 2018

[18] https://health.usnews.com/health-news/articles/2014/06/04/camels-confirmed-as-source-of-human-mers-infection cited 5 May, 2018

Muhammad said: "When you eat, do not wipe your hand till you have licked it, or had it licked by somebody else" (al-Bukhārī 7:366). However, this could result in passing on such saliva-borne diseases, as gastroenteritis, hepatitis A, glandular fever, herpes, respiratory infections and parasites such as giardia. In Muhammad's time, of course, these diseases, although present, had not been identified. But it does raise the question of the applicability of Muhammad's instructions for Muslim communities today.

Further, some of the statements in the Hadith are anatomically incorrect. For example, Muhammad said: (in Sahih Muslim vol. 3 no. 513), "A believer eats in one intestine whereas a non-believer eats in seven intestines." This description does not accord with the realities of the internal organs of non-Muslims. It may have been meant metaphorically, to indicate that non-Muslims ate more than Muslims or were greedier than Muslims, but no evidence for these assertions has been given.

Another qualification for authentic sayings of Muhammad was that they should "not promise large rewards or grave punishments for insignificant acts". However, some hadith appear to defy these standards. In one account, a Jewish prostitute gave water to a thirsty dog. Muhammad commented (in Sahih al-Bukhārī 4:673) that "Allah thanked her for her (good) deed and forgave her" and "Allah approved of her deed and made her enter Paradise." This would seem to be an inordinate reward for a single act. On the other hand, according to Sahih al-Bukhārī 1:712; 3:552, 553, another woman was sent to hell for tying up her cat which subsequently died of thirst. Her punishment for this act was eternal laceration by the cat's claws – a harsh punishment for a single act.

It is hadith accounts about women that have gained attention from feminists and others. A selection of some of Muhammad's reported sayings about women in the Hadith is listed below:

- *Passing a group of women at a praying place, Muhammad commented: "I have not seen anyone more deficient in intelligence and religion than you. A cautious sensible man could be led astray by some of you." The women asked, "O Allah's Apostle! What is deficient in our intelligence and religion?" He said, "Is not the evidence of two women equal to the witness of one man?" They replied in the affirmative. He said, "This is the deficiency in her intelligence. Isn't it true that a woman can neither pray nor fast during her menses?" The women replied in the affirmative. He said, "This is the deficiency in her religion" (al-Bukhārī 1:301).*

38

- *Another time, Allah's Apostle said, "Treat women nicely, for a woman is created from a rib, and the most curved portion of the rib is its upper portion, so, if you should try to straighten it, it will break, but if you leave it as it is, it will remain crooked. So treat women nicely." (al-Bukhārī 4:548). Later, Muhammed invited men to exploit this defect: "So if you want to get benefit from her, do so while she still has some crookedness"* (al-Bukhārī 7:113).

- Women were described as a source of bad luck. Allah's Apostle said, "If at all there is bad omen, it is in the horse, the woman, and the house." (al-Bukhārī 7:32). "Consequently," he continued, "they are men's greatest hardship." The Prophet said, "After me I have not left any affliction more harmful to men than women" (al-Bukhārī 7:33). The Prophet claimed this was due to their propensity to be disloyal to their men: "But for the Israelis, meat would not decay and but for Eve, wives would never betray their husbands" (al–Bukhari 4:547).

- While Muslim men's desires are considered paramount, women's desires are not taken seriously. Normally to enter into a business contract, both partners need to indicate their willingness to do so by either written or verbal means. However to agree to a marriage, a woman need not say anything. When asked how a virgin could indicate her consent to be married, Muhammad said: "Her silence means her consent." (al-Bukhārī 9:79,100,101; 7:67, 68). The reason for this ruling may be a concern about the men hearing a woman's voice. Muhammad said: "The saying 'Sub Han Allah' ['Glory be to God'] is for men and clapping is for women." (If something happens in the prayer, the men can invite the attention of the Imam by saying, "Sub Han Allah". And women, by clapping their hands). Sahih Al-Bukhārī 2:295. The Hadith commentator Ibn Hajar Al-Asqalani concludes that this is because the men should not hear the woman's voice.[19] It is significant that for such an important decision as marriage, the woman's voice need not be heard.

---

[19] Bulugh Al-Maram : Arabic/English Page 81 Hadith 174:
http://www.muhajabah.com/docstorage/voice-amina-h.htm cited 5th May, 2018

- Clearly the husband was to have the dominant role in the marriage: "The Prophet (peace be upon him) said, 'Had it been permissible that a person may prostrate himself before another, I would have ordered that a wife should prostrate herself before her husband'" (al-Tirmidhi 110).

- Women, along with dogs and donkeys, could invalidate men's prayers simply by walking in front of them: "Aisha narrated: The things [Muhammad said] which annul prayers were mentioned before me. They said: 'Prayer is annulled by a dog, a donkey and a woman (if they pass in front of the praying people).' I said: 'You have made us (i.e. women) dogs'" (al-Bukhārī 1:490).

- Women cannot be successful rulers. Muhammad said: "Never will succeed such a nation that makes a woman their ruler" (al-Bukhārī 5:709; 9:219).

- Due to their sins and shortcoming, most of the occupants of hell are female. Muhammad said: "I looked into hell and saw that most of its inhabitants were women" (al-Bukhārī 7:125; 8:456). Another account says: "I saw hell also. No such (abominable) sight have I ever seen as that which I saw today; and I observed that most of its inhabitants were women" (Muslim 1982). Islam's prophet gave women advice on what they should do in the meantime: "You women should give alms even if it consists of your jewellery, for you will be the majority of the inhabitants of *Jahannam* (i.e. hell) on the Day of Resurrection" (al-Tirmidhi 573).

Many female commentators are outraged by such statements. Some deny that Muhammad ever made them. Pakistani scholar Riffat Hassan dismisses any Hadith, including some from al-Bukhārī, which denigrate women. She writes: "It is gratifying to know that these *ahadith* cannot be the words of the Prophet of Islam … [r]egardless of how male chauvinist Muslims project their androcentrism and misogyny on their Prophet". (Hassan "Made from Adam's Rib", p124)

However, to take such an approach would result in a "Swiss-cheese" hadith collection, with parts removed according to the predilection of the commentator. There needs to be some sort of agreement among Muslim scholars as to which hadith should be accepted as authentic and why. Facing this challenge, some Muslims have called for a review of the hadith. In 2008, Turkey's Department of Religious Affairs commissioned a team of theologians at Ankara University to develop a new Hadith collection to assess some of the hadith reports which are not in keeping with the modern world.

Dr Suliman Bashear (1947–1991), a professor at University of Nablus in the West Bank, was clear that some of the hadith are dubious. He said that "serious doubts could easily be cast not only against traditions attributed to the Prophet and Companions but a great deal of those bearing the names of successors too." Others have moved beyond questioning the hadith or even trying to redeem some of them to a wholesale rejection of all hadith. This is not just a new idea, nor one emanating from Western Muslims. A group called *Ahle Qur'an* (People of the Qur'an) was formed in Amritsar and Lahore in 1906, both of which were part of British India at that time. An early leader, Khwaja Ahmad Din (1917), proclaimed boldly: "No hadith can be trusted." His proposals were further developed by others, including Abdullah Chakralawi (d.1930).

The followers of the *Ahle Qur'an* "Qur'an-only" movement base their position on the teachings of the Islamic holy scripture. The Qur'an makes great claims about itself. It describes itself as: 'a light' (from God) (Q.5:15; 7:203; 42:52); a 'clear light' (Q.4:174); 'glorious' (Q.85:21); 'certain' (Q.69:51); 'inspired' (Q.10:2,109; 42:52); 'powerful, unassailable' (Q.41:41); 'wise' (Q.10:1; 31:2; 36:2); 'the truth' (Q.32:3; 35:31; 69:51) and 'perfected in reliability' (Q.6:115).

The Qur'an also speaks of its internal clarity, stating that it is a 'perspicuous/plain book or Qur'an' (Q. 5:15, 12:1; 15:1; 26:2, 195; 27:1; 28:2; 36:69; 43:2; 44:2) with 'clear verses' (Q. 22:16, 24:34, 66:11). Q. 2:242 states that Allah made His signs clear so you can understand. "We (Allah) sent down/made an Arabic Qur'an so that you may understand" (Q. 12:2; 43:3) "in a clear Arabic tongue" (Q. 16:103; 26:195; 20:113; 39:28; 41:3,44; 42:7). The Quranists ask: "If the Qur'an is such a perfect and clear book, why should we look to any another set of literature?"

The Qur'an also claims to be comprehensive. It is "a detailed book" (Q. 6:114) and "a detailed explanation of everything" (Q. 12:111). This "exposition of everything" (Q. 16:89) "has neglected or omitted nothing" (Q. 6:38). Clearly such a book requires nothing else to be added. Nor does it need any explanation, for it provides its own commentary. In the Qur'an, Allah says that "We have explained everything (in detail) with full explanation" (Q. 17:12; 7:52), and "We have sent it down as a Qur'an in Arabic and have explained therein in detail the warnings" (Q. 20:113). In addition, it contains linguistic devices which make it easier to understand: "We have set forth for mankind, in this Qur'an every kind of parable" (Q. 30:58; 39:27), and "indeed We have fully explained to mankind in this Qur'an every kind of similitude" (Q. 17:89; 18:54). Further, the author has sublime credentials: "It is explained by One who is wise and all-knowing" (Q. 11:1).

According to the Qur'an, Allah has done everything to make His book accessible to all, "We made the Qur'an easy to remember" (Q. 54:17, 22, 32, 40; 44:58), particularly to the first recipients: "We made it easy in Muhammad's language" (Q. 19:97; 44:58). Facilitating His message to humanity has always been a concern of Allah. He is quoted as saying: "We did not send a messenger except with the language of his people" (Q. 14:4). Likewise, Muhammad was to convey the message clearly (Q. 16:82) so he "can lead people out of darkness into light" (Q. 14:1) through its clear signs or verses (Q. 22:16; 24:46; 57:9). To underline the sufficiency of the Qur'an, it states that Allah could have supplied other books if needed (Q. 18:109). So, the argument for the adequacy of the Qur'an is strong. If the Qur'an is as great, clear, comprehensive, fully explained, uncomplicated, and sufficient as it claims, why should other books be needed?

The mere existence of the hadith casts doubts on these claims of the Qur'an. The Egyptian-American activist, Ahmed Subhi Mansour (b.1949) formed an organisation named *Ahl al-Qur'an* ("People of the Qur'an") organisation to:

> *unify all those who believe that Qur'an is the ONLY source of Islam rituals, guidance and explanation of its legislations. So, it will be*

42

forbidden for anyone who adopts what-so-called Prophet Narrations (Hadith or Sunnah) to be used or adopted to express certain point of view or interpret the Holy Qur'an.[20]

Another Qur'an-only group, which calls itself 'Free-Minds.org' claims:

[t]he gravest crime the self-appointed scholars who claimed to be Muslim made was to give authority to the traditions (Sunna) and the books of Sayings (Hadith) ALONGSIDE the authority of God and His messenger (emphasis theirs).[21]

The highest profile opponent of the hadith was Libyan dictator Colonel Mu'ammar Qaddafi. In 1977, he noted the hadith attributed to Muhammad which said: "When two Muslims fight (meet) each other with their swords, both the murderer as well as the murdered will go to the Hell-fire" (al-Bukhārī 1:30). He stated that many Muslims, including members of Muhammad's only family such as his son-in-law Ali and Muhammad's own grandsons Hassan and Hussein had fought in wars against other Muslims. According to this hadith, they would be in hell-fire. He consequently announced publicly that he no longer accepted any hadith as authoritative. He was visited by members of the radical group *Hizb Ut-Tahrir* and then by Al-Azhar's Sheikh Muhammad al-Gazoly who told him that if he continued to hold this position he would no longer be counted as a Muslim. As a result, he recanted and repented.

It is the internal contradictions in the hadith themselves, such as this one, and the scientific and women's rights issues recounted above, as well the external problems that they raise about the adequacy of the Qur'an that present some significant problems for Muslims. Without the hadith, Muslims would not know how many times a day to pray, or how to wash, or whether to circumcise, for these important details are missing from the Qur'an. But when the door is opened to accept the wildly contradictory, and in some cases, the socially and intellectually untenable concepts which are taught in the hadith, then Muslims find themselves caught on the horns of a difficult-to-resolve dilemma.

---

[20] http://ahl-alquran.com/English/terms.php 5th May, 2018

[21] https://www.free-minds.org/god-alone cited 5th May, 2018

PROBLEMS WITH THE QUR'AN ORIGIN STORY

Mark Durie

Islam as a faith is based on canonical texts held sacred by Muslims. Its canon has two main components. One is the *Qur'an*, the text of which goes back at least to the lifetime of Muhammad. This is Islam's oldest and first canonical text. The other component of the Islamic canon is the *Sunnah*, an Arabic word meaning 'path', which refers to the pattern of Muhammad's words and deeds.

There is a traditional Islamic story about the origin of the Qur'an, that its text was 'sent down' to Muhammad during his lifetime in segments. However, there are several problems with that story, and we will review some of these problems here. 'Revisionist' scholars have been suggesting alternative explanations for the origin of the Qur'an since the second half of the 20th century. We will not be able to survey all these alternatives here, but instead will review some issues or problems with the official explanation for the origins of the Qur'an.

What is offered here is not intended to be a cutting-edge research article. Rather it is a written version of a talk, originally prepared for a conference on 'Understanding and Answering Islam'. What is written here is intended for a broader audience than scholarly experts in the area of the origins of the Qur'an. In some respects this presentation simplifies what is a very complex and rapidly developing field. Some of the ideas presented will be well known to researchers: others represent ideas which may be less familiar.

Let us first consider, in brief, the received Islamic account of the origin of the Qur'an.

45

The Muhammad Story

In Islam, the context for reading and understanding the Qur'an is supplied by Sunnah. The Sunnah was preserved for posterity and passed down to us in the form of *hadith*, or traditions about Muhammad's life, which tell us of Muhammad and his companions' words and deeds. Sunni Muslims generally recognise six collections of Hadiths as canonical.

Augmenting the hadith collections as sources on the *Sunnah* are biographies of Muhammad, the *sirah*, which strictly speaking can be considered to be made up of traditions arranged in chronological order.

What we know of the life of Muhammad, which is the grid through which most Muslims read and interpret the Qur'an, is based on the hadiths and *sirah*.

According to the traditional account of Islam's origins, Muhammad, the son of Abdullah, was born c. 570 CE and died in 632 CE. His family belonged to a Meccan tribe, the Quraysh. Muhammad's fellow tribespeople were initially opposed to the religion he was preaching, so after enduring persecution Muhammad and his small band of dedicated followers migrated to Medina in 622, by which time he was around 52 years old. After this migration violent hostilities commenced between Muslims and non-Muslims, but Muhammad's followers grew in strength, until the day came when Muhammad's army advanced on Mecca and he was able to conquer his home town without a fight. Subsequently, Muslim armies spread far and wide to extent the rule of Islam.

According to the traditions, revelations and segments of what became the Qur'an, began to be received by Muhammad through the angel Jibril when Muhammad was around 40 years old (around 610 CE). The traditions also report that Qur'an verses were initially received, recited and passed on in oral, not written form. At a certain point Muhammad would receive a verse, or a longer passage, which he would communicate to his followers through recitation. They then kept these verses in their memory until they were committed to writing. According to Sunni tradition, the text of the Qur'an was consolidated under Abu Bakr (d. 634 CE), the first Caliph, not long after Muhammad died. He did this by appointing a team to review and compare all the written and memorised variants of the text available to them.

Sometime around 650 to 655 CE, approximately 20 years after its initial collation in written form, the quranic text was standardised again by order of the third Caliph Uthman. According to tradition, at that time all extant versions except one were deliberately destroyed by burning, and multiple copies of the authorised version were made and distributed throughout the Islamic empire.

This, in a nutshell, is the standard account of the origins of Islam and the Qur'an.

We will now note some of the issues with this origin story.

The Problem of the Time Gap between Muhammad and the Traditions

In evaluating the reliability of Islam's origins story, the timing and dates of the sources are significant. The canonical hadith collections were compiled, and their text fixed, around 230 to 300 years after Muhammad. The earliest surviving biography, the *Sirat Rasul Allah* of Ibn Ishaq, was written around 150 years after Muhammad, but the version we have was redacted by Ibn Hisham half a century after its composition (Guillaume 1955). The authorship of our oldest written records of the life of Muhammad dates back no earlier than c. 150 years after his death.

I personally remember the Beatles' visit to Australia in 1964, and the Beatles are part of the living memory of millions of others besides me, even more than half a century after they became famous. If someone were to write a history of the Beatles today they would be narrating events which involve many people who are alive, and what they write could be subjected to the test of living memories. However, if someone were to compose a narrative about events that date back 150 to 300 years before the present, such as, for example, a biography of Lincoln (d. 1865), Napoleon (d. 1821) or the composer Handel (d. 1759) this would reach back multiple generations, going well beyond living memory. Yet this is the extent of time between when Muhammad is reported to have lived, and the period when Muslims were compiling the canonical documentation of his life and teaching. The records of the example and teaching of Muhammad which have been passed down to us were committed to writing by people for whom the events they were relating had passed well beyond living memory.

This time gap is significant. In contrast, the gospels were written in the first century CE, for the most part within living memory of the events they report. In contrast, the story of Islam's origins relies on documents which were composed generations after the events they relate. This makes them questionable historical sources.

Issues with "Muhammad" as the Messenger of the Qur'an: External Evidence

The main human protagonist of the Qur'an is normally referred to in the Qur'an itself as 'the messenger', and less frequently as 'the prophet'. The personal name by which the quranic messenger has come to be known is Muhammad, which in Arabic means 'praised one'.

It is a puzzle that this name is only mentioned 4 times in the Qur'an. Why would the founder of Islam be mentioned by name so few times? Why would a book whose contents centre around one particular person 'the Messenger' only mention this person by name 4 times? (By way of contrast the name 'Jesus' is mentioned more than a thousand times in the four gospels.)

Moreover, when the word *Muhammad* is mentioned, it is also not clear whether it is a personal name, or a title meaning 'the praised one'. The Qur'an also has a single reference to a figure called *Ahmad* 'most praised one', who Jesus says will come after him (Q61:6). Here again the question arises: is *Ahmad* to be read as a name or a title? The similarity in meaning between Muhammad and Ahmad as '(most) praised one' could suggest that both were titles rather than names.

We have already noted the considerable gap of 150-300 years between the traditional dating of the life of Muhammad and the committing to writing of the hadiths and *sirah* in the form they have been passed down to us. Are there other independent early sources which could help to confirm the existence of a historical figure called Muhammad? Or of Islam, the religion he brought?

48

As it happens, non-Muslim sources offer little awareness of a distinct Islamic faith in the first century of Islam, from 630--730. The words *Islam* and *Muslim* are not attested in non-Muslim sources until the second century of Islam. There are references to conquering Arabs in contemporary sources, but the conquerors are referred to variously as pagans, Saracens, Hagarenes, and Ishmaelites. They are not called Muslims until the second Islamic century.

Arabs habitually wrote graffiti on rocks, leaving many thousands of examples, and it is striking that the name Muhammad is not recorded in any datable rock inscriptions until the second Islamic century, in 730--31 CE (Nevo and Koren: 199). There are early monotheistic inscriptions from the early 7th century CE, but these make no mention of the name Muhammad.

The earliest coin to bear an inscription naming Muhammad dates from 685–689 CE (Heidemann 2011: 167). However, the name Muhammad is rarely mentioned by non-Muslims until the second Islamic century. The earliest dateable references to the name Muhammad in Christian Syriac sources come from the two decades after Muhammad's death, in 637 CE and 640 CE, but they seem to refer to a living leader of Arab armies, not the (by then) dead founder of a religion.[1] There is also a reference in a Greek text to a false prophet amongst the Saracens, but again in reference to a living leader.[2] The next Christian reference to Muhammad is by John bar Penkaye, dated 687 CE, but here he is identified as a teacher of a legal tradition (Penn 2015: 92; Hoyland 1997: 196).

The external contemporary evidence points to an Arab leader, but it is inconsistent with Islam's own sources that what evidence there is points to a leader who was still alive in the 630's.

---

[1] Two relatively early Syriac references to Muḥammad date to 637 CE and 640 CE, and there is a reference in the Khuzistan Chronicle of c 660 CE which states: 'their leader was Muḥammad' (Penn 2015: 23–24, 28, 49).

[2] The *Doctrina Jacobi nuper baptizati*, dated 634 CE states that 'a false prophet has appeared among the Saracens' (Crone & Cook 1977, 3–4; Nevo & Koren 2003, 208).

The Issue of the Reliability of the Hadiths and *Sirah* Literature: Internal Evidence

The traditions or hadiths, together with the biographies, are the foundation on which the official account of the origin of the Qur'an rests. We have also noted that there is a considerable time gap between the lifetime of the Muhammad, and the committing to writing of these biographical materials, and this is one of the problems with Islam's origin story.

A question to be considered is: how well do the Qur'an and the traditions actually connect with each other? Do they offer conflicting or complementary perspectives?

Many authors have pointed out that there are inconsistencies between the hadiths and the *sirah* on the one hand, and the Qur'an on the other. Already in the 19th century Goldziher in *Muhammedanische Studien* commented that:

> *A more thorough acquaintance with the enormous corpus of 'aḥādith' [the hadiths] should lead us to skeptical caution rather than optimistic trust with regard to the materials amassed into scrupulously compiled collections. … we consider the overwhelmingly greater part of it to be the result of religious, historical and social developments of Islam in the first two centuries. The 'aḥādith' cannot serve as (source) documents for the history of the childhood of Islam; instead they reflect the influence of aspirations which emerged in the community during its maturer stages of development.* (Goldziher 1888–1890, 2:5)

In essence Goldziher is saying that materials which provide the biography of Muhammad, including the traditions, were constructed to address religious issues which arose in the Islamic community well after Muhammad's death.

This opinion has been reinforced by subsequent researchers. H. Lammens (1910) concluded that the biographies of Muhammad were generated by the needs of quranic exegesis, and Joseph Schacht (1967) developed this idea further in his research into the foundations of Islamic jurisprudence, concluding that the vast body of traditions about Muhammad and his companions were put into circulation towards the end of the 2nd century after Muhammad, in order to support a pre-existing body of law:

> *The traditions from the Prophet and his Companions do not contain more or less authentic information on the earliest period of Islam to*

which they claim to belong, but reflect opinions held during the first
two and a half centuries after the hijra. (Schacht 1949, 143)

In an important recent study, Gerald Hawting (2015) has argued that passages in *Sura* 8 of the Qur'an which are thought by Islamic tradition to refer to the battle of Badr, an event described in the *sirah*, cannot be reconciled with the *sirah* sources. His conclusion is that the linking of the battle of Badr narrative with *Sura* 8 is spurious:

> Even allowing for the typically allusive and elliptical Quranic style, reading much of *Sūrat al-Anfāl* [Q8] as a series of references to the battle of Badr involves an interpretation that hardly seems to arise from the text itself. (Hawting 2015: 91)

The Quranic Text: Divine Dictation or Human Performance?

In an important recent study, Andrew Bannister (2014) has argued that the text of the Qur'an has a linguistic structure which could only have been produced by a skilled oral performer, who was in the habit of regularly addressing an audience by extemporizing performed recitations. Bannister's argument rests upon the high degree of repetition of formulaic material within the Qur'an, which reflects the *modus operandi* of a skilled oral performer. The highly formulaic linguistic structure is inconsistent with the traditional Islamic understanding that the Qur'an was a compilation of individual passages revealed in diverse contexts over many years, which were only gathered into chapters later. Instead the Qur'an's structure points to it being produced in the context of performances before an audience. Some, but not all, of these performances were written down and preserved, being incorporated into the Qur'an. There is an inconsistency between the oral performance character of the text of the Qur'an, and the idea that Muhammad was receiving individual verses or groups of verses in diverse contexts throughout his life, which were only subsequently stitched together into chapters.

The evidence adduced by Bannister implies that the Qur'an's *suras* could only be created in an oral performance tradition which would have taken decades to develop, and the skill of producing performances of this kind would have taken a long time for a performer to master. Based on evidence from other contexts, maintaining such a performance tradition would normally involve a community of performers.

We can note that Bannister's conclusions align with the meaning of the Arabic word *qur'an* 'recitation, lectionary', which points to a text intended for recitation in a formal mode of public performance.

The Arabic of the Qur'an is a Settled Urban Variety, Not a Bedouin Dialect

The form of Arabic the Qur'an is written in presents another set of problems. The official history of the Qur'an would imply that it was originally composed in the dialect of the Arabs of Mecca, as both Muhammad and his audience would have been native speakers of this dialect. However we know from early Muslim grammarians, who carefully investigated all the Arab dialects known to them, that the Qur'an was not composed in the Meccan dialect of the Quraysh, or in any other single Bedouin dialect which they were able to identify. Indeed they concluded that Allah had revealed the Qur'an in a multiplicity of dialects, because its linguistic features seemed to have correspondences in many dialects, without being identifiable as any one particular dialect (Rabin 1955).

At the time when the Qur'an was being produced, Arabs were distinguished into two groups – there were nomadic desert dwellers (the Bedouin) and settled groups of agriculturalists and town dwellers. Bedouin nomads were considered to be pure Arabs, in contrast to Arabs who had settled down to an agricultural means of subsistence, such as the Nabataeans.

Based on recent research it has become clear that the Arabic of the quranic script is consistent with a settled dialect, spoken across the region of Nabataean influence, the southern Levant. It is not the Arabic of Bedouin nomads. The strongest evidence for this identification comes from Arabic materials written in Greek letters in the centuries just before the Qur'an appeared. The Graeco-Arabic of the southern Levant was recently surveyed by Al-Jallad (2017). There are additionally a large number of rock inscriptions of various nomadic Arabic dialects, from before the appearance of Islam (see e.g. Al-Jallad 2017), but none of these aligns with the dialect of the Qur'an. Three linguistic features which distinguish quranic Arabic from the dialects of Arab nomads are the use of –*h* instead of -*t* for the feminine ending, the form of the definite article *al-* (without assimilation of the following consonant), and the loss of case endings.[3] As Al-Jallad's research into Graeco-Arabic has shown, these are all features of the Arabic spoken in the Nabataean sphere of influence in the southern Levant.[4]

It has long been recognised that the Arabic script used to write the Qur'an was developed from Nabatean Aramaic script. The Nabateans were Arabic native speakers who lived in Petra, conducted agriculture by means of irrigation, and controlled an extensive trade network. It seems clear that the emergence of written Arabic, which was taking place in the two centuries immediately before the Qur'an was written down, developed out of the Nabataeans' use of Aramaic. Moreover it is becoming apparent that the spelling conventions and probably even the dialect in which the Qur'an is written align with features of Nabataen Arabic, not of a Bedouin dialect spoken in Mecca.

The Apocalypse and Plate Tectonics
The Qur'an is very concerned with eschatology, with the end of the world, and also with intermediate judgements of Allah visited upon communities. In *suras* produced in the earlier part of the Messenger's prophetic career, he is prophesying imminent catastrophic judgement in this life on disbelievers. He repeatedly recites stories of how this has happened in the past to other peoples through earthquake, inundation, wind, fire from the heavens and other acts of God. The Messenger repeatedly points his hearers to ruins where communities who were destroyed by Allah in the past used to live, and urges his listeners to repent lest they suffer destruction too. Some took the Messenger's threat of divine judgement to heart, and believed his message, but others began to mock him, saying, in effect 'bring it on'. This skeptical response is what the Qur'an refers to as 'hurrying the punishment' (Q. 29:53–54; Q. 37:176).

---

[3] The Arabic term for these case endings is *'i'rāb*, which is derived from *'a'rāb* 'Bedouin Arab', because the case endings were associated with Bedouin speech.

[4] Conventions developed well after the Qur'an was written for its recitation in some respects hypercorrected the text to conform it more closely to Bedouin varieties, for example by the addition of case endings, and assimilation of the *al-* article to following 'sun' consonants.

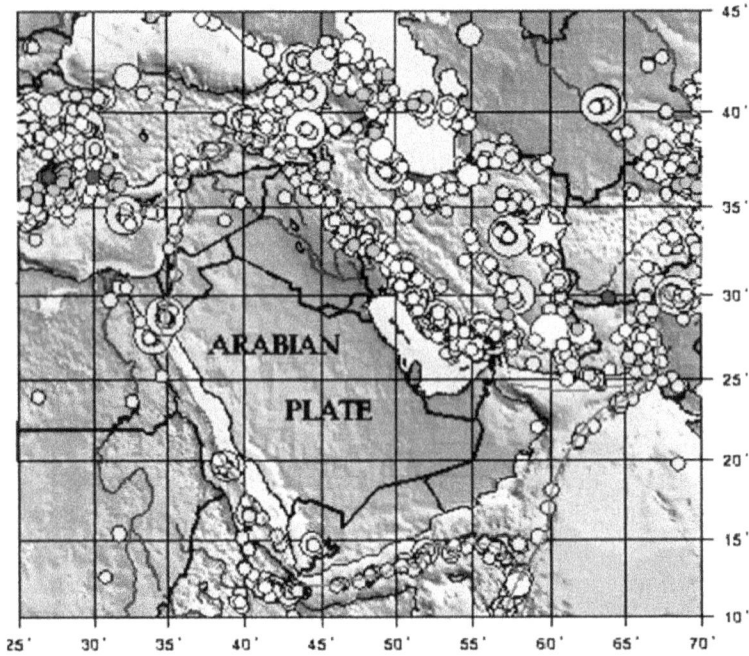

Arabian Tectonic Plate
Seismicity 1962-1997 Earthquakes Magnitude 5.0 or greater
(Reproduced from <http://earthquake.usgs.gov> US Earthquake Hazards Program)
Credit: U.S. Geological Survey, Department of the Interior/USGS

These observations raise the intriguing question of what could have been a plausible context for promoting a message of imminent catastrophe? The most receptive environment would be one in which there was a memory of major catastrophes in living memory.

At it happens, communities in the region to the north of Arabia had experienced devastating natural disasters in the centuries leading up to the time when the Qur'an was first being recited. In particular, the Jordan Rift Valley, which includes the Arabah Wadi, and stretches up through the Dead Sea to the Sea of Gallilee towards Beirut, is highly subject to earthquakes (see above map[5]).

---

[5] Originally viewed at
http://earthquake.usgs.gov/earthquakes/eqarchives/year/1997/1997_05_10_plates.gif
now available at

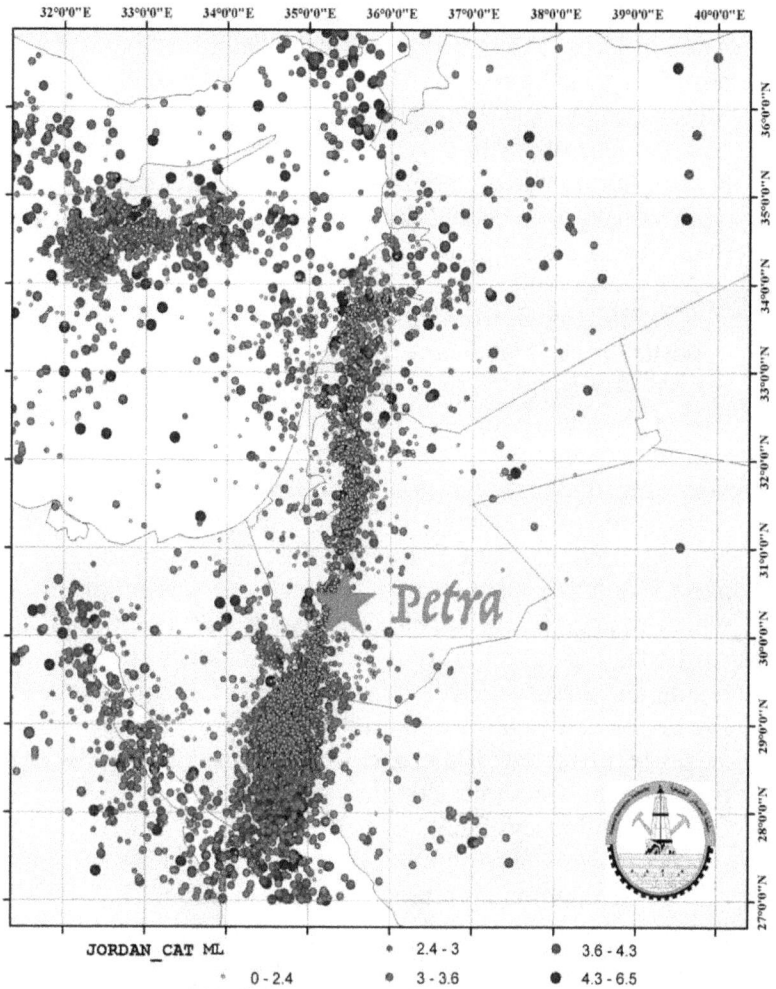

Map labels (left to right, top): 32°0'0"E 33°0'0"E 34°0'0"E 35°0'0"E 36°0'0"E 37°0'0"E 38°0'0"E 39°0'0"E 40°0'0"E

Petra

JORDAN_CAT ML

0 - 2.4	2.4 - 3	3.6 - 4.3
	3 - 3.6	4.3 - 6.5

Earthquake Distribution from 1900 to 2005. Jordan Catalogue.

Earthquakes in the Levant 1900-2005
modified to show the location of Petra

(reproduced from Jreisat and Yazjeen 2014)

(From the *Atlas of Jordan: A Seismic Junction,* Kamal Jreisat and Tawfiq Yazreen, Figure 1.8—Earthquake distribution in Jordan and the Middle East from 1900 to 2005
http://books.openedition.org/ifpo/4861 cited 25 January 2018. Reproduced with permission.)

https
/199

55

On the other hand, the threat of earthquakes or inundation ought to have made little impact in the Arabian Desert, because the Arabian Plate is the most tectonically stable and least earthquake-prone area in the region. There is minimal risk of earthquakes in Mecca and Medina. Furthermore, someone who lives in a tent need have no fear of earthquakes. It is townsfolk living in solidly built homes, not nomads, who have reason to fear earthquakes, because a brick or wooden beam falling on one's head more life-threatening than finding oneself in a collapsed tent.

We know from historical accounts that Petra (see map opposite), the Nabatean capital was repeatedly damaged by earthquakes in the 4th through to the 6th centuries CE. There was a pair of particularly devastating earthquakes on May 18 and 19, 363 CE, which destroyed half of Petra and disrupted its water supply. Widespread damage was also reported from these two quakes across a region stretching up into Galilee. Major earthquakes were also reported for 419 CE and 502 CE. The Antioch earthquake of 526 CE killed approximately 250,000 and was followed by a fire which consumed the whole city. There was also the great Beirut earthquake of July 9, 551 CE, which wreaked havoc across a wide region and also destroyed Petra. This 551 CE earthquake started a fire in Beirut which was reported to have raged for two months, and it was reported that 101 coastal towns and villages were destroyed by a tsunami (previous tsunamis were reported in 306 CE and 502 CE; see Ambraseys 2009).

Muhammad is reported to have been born c. 570 CE, or just twenty years after the devastating earthquake of 551 CE. This devastating earthquake, and associated tsunamis and fires would have been within the living memory of people in the Levant at the time Muhammad was beginning his prophetic career.

A region where there had been major natural disasters in living memory would be the optimal place to preach an apocalyptic message of divine judgement by earthquake, fire or inundation. Furthermore, the association of apocalyptic thought and natural disasters is well documented throughout history. It was also part of the Christian theological expectation that earthquakes would be linked with the end of the world: in Mark 13:8, Luke 21:11 and Matthew 24:8 Jesus speaks of earthquakes as the 'beginning of birth pangs' of the end.

These considerations suggest that the southern Levant would have been a more plausible context for Muhammad to commence his apocalyptic preaching than the deserts of Arabia.

The Agrarian Environment of the Qur'an and the Employment of its Community

Let us turn now from a consideration of plate tectonics to agriculture, and the physical environment of the Qur'an. The Qur'an refers repeatedly to surrounding physical features such as streams, valleys, fields, springs of water, trees, grass, clay and loam, which is formed by the movement of water. It also refers to agriculture involving grains, date palms, grapes, olives, pomegranates, luxuriant gardens, green vegetables, fruits of all kinds and fodder for cattle. The quranic community is described as being busy with various forms of agriculture including growing crops and tending sheep, goats, cattle, camels, horses, mules and donkeys, taking them out to pasture and bringing them back each day. The Messenger keeps telling his audience to contemplate their crops, orchards and livestock, and consider the goodness of Allah to them (Crone 2005).

None of this makes any sense in Mecca or Medina. Furthermore, in the Qur'an the Messenger is criticised by his opponents for not having a garden. When he was preaching about the garden that will come in the next life, some of his audience mocked him for not even owning a garden here on earth. Such a charge could only make sense in a context where cultivation of gardens was possible, but Mecca is not such a place.

So there is a discrepancy between the physical environment described in the Qur'an and the habitual occupation of its residents, and the physical reality of Mecca. Mecca is an unlikely context for the Qur'an.

More Problems with Quranic Geography

Another issue is that most of the place names mentioned in the Qur'an are settlements in the north of Arabia, for example Thamud and Madyan. Yathrib (Medinah) is only mentioned once and Makkah is mentioned only once as well. (Al-Medinah is mentioned several times, but it means 'the town', and the references cannot be conclusively tied to any one place.) It is striking that the two most important places in Muhammad's life story, Mecca and Yathrib (Medinah) are only mentioned once each.

There are also references in the Qur'an to ruins that are readily visible to the Messenger's audience. The audience are said to walk past the ruins of Lot's people, which are not far away, each morning and night (Q. 3:137-138; Q. 11:89; cf. Genesis 19 on Sodom and Gomorrah). However, the location for Sodom and Gomorrah is more than 1,200 kms to the north of Mecca, and there are no such ruins in Mecca.

Another issue is that the Romans are said to have been defeated in the 'nearest part of the land' (Q.30:2-5). There are a number of battles this could refer to, but none of them anywhere near Mecca or Medina. The Byzantines were defeated by the Persians in Jerusalem in 614, and in Damascus in 613, and Byzantine-ruled Petra had fallen to the Persians in 548, but all these places are a long, long way from Mecca, it is not the nearest part of the land.

The Problem of Idolatry

Gerald Hawting's *The Idea of Idolatry and the Emergence of Islam* argues that the references to idolatry in the Qur'an are unlikely to fit a Meccan context:

> ... the picture of pagan worship presented in the Qur'an allegedly of the Meccans is confused, contradictory and lacks verification. The names given in the Qur'an and in Muslim tradition relate to forms relatively well attested over a broad chronological span before Islam, and notably, especially in the north Arabian and Syrian desert region. (Hawting 2006: 142)

The idols of al-Lat, al-Uzza, Manat and Hubal, mentioned in the Qur'an as the daughters of Allah, were widely known Nabataean deities. These were gods of settled Arab communities, not the Bedouin, and the centre of the cult of these goddesses was in the Nabataean-dominated region in the north of Arabia, very much to the north of Mecca and Medina.

The Problem of Manuscripts

There was much media attention given in July 2015 to the dating of some leaves of a Qur'an held in Birmingham, which were originally part of a manuscript now held in Paris. Carbon dating placed the manuscript to between 568 CE and 645 CE, with a 95% probability. This is challenging for the standard account of the origins of the Qur'an. Recall the dates for Muhammad, who lived 570 to 632, and that the text of the Qur'an was reportedly standardised under Utham between 650 and 655 CE. If the Islamic account of the standardization of the Qur'an were true, we should expect manuscripts to date from 650 CE onwards. The window of time between 568 CE and 645 CE stretches from before Muhammad was born, through to a time well before the Uthmanic standardization, when all other previously existing manuscripts copies were allegedly burnt. The 77 year window of this dating overlaps with Muhammad's lifetime. So at first sight this appears to be a manuscript that escaped the fires of Uthman, perhaps even one that Muhammad held in his own hands.

Although this was the manuscript that caught the media's attention, some have even earlier dates. In the Great Mosque of Sana'a in Yemen, a cache of manuscripts was found behind a wall during renovations. Scholars have had the opportunity to examine some of the manuscripts. Six fragments from that cache have been carbon-dated, and the results have been reported by Christian Robin (2015). Two leaves are dated from 543–643 CE, one from 433–599 CE, one from 603–662 CE, and one from 388–535 CE, all within 95% probability. The 388–535 dated fragment was retested by 3 other laboratories giving the results 504–550 CE (1423 ± 23 BP,[6] Oxford), 480–546 CE (1437 ± 33 BP, Zurich), and 410 460 CE (1515 ± 25 BP, Kiel; Robin 2015: 65). All of these dates are too early to align with the received account of Muhammad, who was only reported to have commenced receiving Quranic revelations in 610 CE, and then continued to receive the Qur'an over the following twenty-three years.

It must be born in mind that carbon dating is of the leather parchment on which a text is written, so what is being dated is the time when the sheep was alive. This raises the question of how long parchment was stored before being used. One view is that since parchment was incredibly valuable, it would not have been stored for a long time. A single Qur'an would have required skins from a hillside full of sheep, an expensive proposition indeed. Another possibility is that parchment was sometimes scraped clean and reused. In any case, these dates are startling. What is particularly

---

[6] BP in Carbon dating refers to years before 1950, which is taken as year zero for carbon dating purposes.

troubling is not the existence of one or two exceptionally early dates, but the fact that the centre of the date range for so many samples falls before 610 CE, the year when Muhammad was supposed to have commenced receiving revelations. In many cases, in order to make the manuscript 'fit' Muhammad's dates, it is necessary to prefer dates at the extreme late end of the possible carbon dating range.

These dates are so early that they seem to imply that the Qur'an existed before Muhammad was born. If the name 'Muhammad' was added later, this might help explain why he is only mentioned 4 times, and why Meccah and Yathrib, (Medina) are only mentioned by name once.

An explanation which integrates the quranic dating with early Christian references to Muhammad as a military leader active in the years after Muhammad was supposed to have died, could be that the text of the Qur'an had arisen earlier in the geographical sphere of Nabataean influence, and the original Messenger was not Muhammad at all. It only later became associated with the name of the military leader Muhammad. This association could have served a political purpose, providing a religious ideology for the emerging Arab kingdom, which was being formed by conquests.

Nevertheless, to suggest a theory like this begs a thousand questions. It is certainly well beyond the scope of this chapter to propose a serious alternative to the received account of the origin of the Qur'an, and it would be extraordinarily ambitious to develop a theory which could account for all the problematic data. Our concern here is to not to solve the perplexing question of the origins of the Qur'an, but to note the many problems with the received account of how the Qur'an came to be.

Conclusions

The traditional story the history of the Qur'an, according to Islamic tradition, is that the Qur'an was sent down to Muhammad in segments over 23 years. According to Islamic tradition, Muhammad was a poor member of a large Meccan tribe, he was not highly educated, and he was not an urban Arab. The dialect of Arabic he spoke as his native tongue would have been the dialect of his family. It would not have been the Arabic of urban settlements hundreds of kilometres to the north in which the Qur'an was written.

According to the Qur'an, the Messenger began his prophetic career by warning of imminent apocalyptic destruction. That is not something that Arabs living in the desert would have any concerns about. However, to the north, where many communities had been destroyed within living memory by earthquakes, bringing inundation through tsunamis and devestating fires, such a message would have been much more likely to gain traction.

Furthermore, the Qur'an speaks as if the Meccas were living in the vicinity of ruins of previous civilisations, yet such ruins do not exist near Mecca and Medina. The geography does not fit. The variety of Arabic does not fit. The physical environment does not fit. The manuscript dating does not fit.

There is an alternative story to be told but exactly what this story should be is far from clear. One of the psychological challenges is that the Mecca-Medina origins story for the Qur'an, the received story of the life of Muhammad, has become so dominant in the way that people think about the Qur'an, that it has become very difficult to entertain and explore alternatives. Nevertheless, discussions of issues such as have been canvassed here have been going on for a long time in scholarly circles, and it is a mark of the rarified nature of Qur'anic studies that much of this material has yet to work its way into popular consciousness. In part this reflects the wall that is put around Muhammad as the prophet of Islam. To criticise or challenge the Muhammad myth is perceived by many within Islam to be a personal attack on Islam and Muslims.

Of course, it goes without saying that most ordinary Muslims have no idea of any of this material. They don't study the Qur'an and Meccan geography to try to piece together how the Meccans could possibly have raised cattle and grown crops in Mecca, which they must have if the received account of quranic origins was correct.

Islam's system of spiritual authority is structured in such a way that an individual believer is encouraged to find someone more knowledgable than they, and to follow their teachings. In Islam individuals are held accountable before Allah for obeying what someone more knowledgeable than they has taught them. They are not held accountable for analysing the religion critically. Individual believers are not encouraged, equipped or empowered to ask fundamental questions which might cast doubt on the fundamental verities of Islam, such as the Muhammad story.

There are other puzzles about the Muhammad story: we have considered only some of them here. I hope to have provided something of a taste of the considerable ferment that quranic studies finds itself in, and of the seriousness of the many open issues surrounding the birth pangs of the Islamic faith, and in particular of the origin story of the Qur'an.

References

Ambraseys, Nicholas. 2009. *Earthquakes in the Eastern Mediterranean and the Middle East.* Cambridge: CUP.

Bannister, Andrew G. 2014. *An Oral-Formulaic Study of the Qur'an.* Plymouth: Lexington Books.

Crone, Patricia. 2005. "How Did the Quranic Pagans Make a Living?" *Bulletin of the School of Oriental and African Studies* 68(3): 387–99.

Crone, Patricia, and Michael A. Cook. 1977. *Hagarism: The Making of the Islamic World.* Cambridge: CUP.

Goldziher, Ignaz. 1888–1890. *Muhammedanische Studien.* Halle: Niemeyer.

Guillaume, A. 1955. *The Life of Muhammad: A Translation of Ibn Ishaq's Sirat Rasul Allah.* Karachi & Oxford: OUP.

Hawting, Gerald R. 2015. "Qur' ā n and Sī rah: The Relationship Between Sū rat Al-Anfā l and Muslim Traditional Accounts of the Battle of Badr." In *Les Origines Du Coran: Le Coran Des Origines*, edited by François Déroche, Christian Julien Robin, and Michel Zink, 75–91. Académie des Inscriptions et Belles-Lettres.

Heidemann, Stefan. 2011. "The Evolving Representation of the Early Islamic Empire and its Religion on Coin Imagery." In *The Qur' ān in Context: Historical and Literary Investigations into the Qur'ānic Milieu*, edited by Angelika Neuwirth, Nicolai Sinai, and Michael Marx, 149–96. Leiden: Brill.

Hoyland, Robert G. 1997. *Seeing Islam as Others Saw it: A Survey and Evaluation of Christian, Jewish and Zoroastrian Writings on Early Islam*. Princeton, N.J.: The Darwin Press.

Al-Jallad, Ahmad. 2015. *An Outline of the Grammar of the Safaitic Inscriptions*. Leiden: Brill.

———. 2017. "Graeco-Arabic I: The Southern Levant." In *Arabic in Context*, edited by Ahmad Al-Jallad, 99–186. Louvain: Brill.

Jreisat, Kamal, and Tawfiq Yazjeen. 2014. "A Seismic Junction." In *Atlas of Jordan*, edited by Myriam Ababsa, 47–59. Beirut: l'Institut français du Proche-Orient.

Lammens, H. 1910. "Qoran et tradition: Comment fut composé la vie de Mahomet." *Recherches de Science Religieuse* 1 25–51.

Nevo, Yehuda D., and Judith Koren. 2003. *Crossroads to Islam: The Origins of the Arab Religion and the Arab State*. Amherst, NY: Prometheus Books.

Penn, Michael Philip. 2015. *When Christians First Met Muslims: A Sourcebook of the Earliest Syriac Writings on Islam*. Oakland: University of California Press.

Rabin, Chaim. 1955. "The Beginnings of Classical Arabic." *Studia Islamica* 4: 19–37.

Robin, Christian Julien. 2015. "L'arabie Dans Le Coran: Réexamen De Quelques Termes À La Lumière Des Inscriptions Préislamiques." In *Les Origines Du Coran: Le Coran Des Origines*, edited by François Déroche, Christian Julien Robin, and Michel Zink, 27–76. Académie des Inscriptions et Belles-Lettres.

Schacht, Joseph. 1949. 1967. *The Origins of Muhammadan Jurisprudence*. 4th ed. Oxford: Clarendon Press.

UNDERSTANDING WITHOUT ANSWERING, ANSWERING WITHOUT UNDERSTANDING:

The case of *Tafsir*

Peter Riddell

For centuries, apologetics was the method of choice by Christians engaging with Muslims. Within a century of the death of Muhammad, John of Damascus, the last of the Church Fathers, had fine-tuned the art of Christian apologetics to Islam to a point where it was very quickly to become the mainstream approach.[1] Between John's death in 749AD and the great debate in Agra between Carl Pfander and Khairanawi in 1854,[2] a steady stream of Christian apologists sought to build on arguments developed by their forebears in ever-better ways, seeking for that silver bullet that would answer the challenge of Islam and assert the truth of Christianity in the process. Granted, there were voices during those 11 centuries seeking alternative methods. The much-quoted case of St Francis of Assisi crossing the battle lines to speak with Sultan Al-Kamil during the 5th crusade showed that alternative methodologies were around.[3] But they were not mainstream.

However, the last 150 years have witnessed a sea-change in Christian methods of engagement with Muslims. In many quarters apologetics has become very unfashionable, even unacceptable.

---

[1] Cf. D. Janosik, *John of Damascus: First Apologist to the Muslims*, Eugene, OR:Pickwick Publications, 2016.

[2] Cf. J. Smith, *The Life, Work & Legacy of Carl Pfander, 19th Century Apologist to Islam*, PhD dissert., Australian College of Theology, 2017.

[3] Cf. P. Moses, *The Saint and the Sultan: The Crusades, Islam, and Francis of Assisi's Mission of Peace*, Crown Publishing Group, 2009.

The quest to "understand" Islam has come to the fore. Centres for Christian-Muslim Understanding (or similar names) are emerging in increasing numbers.[4] Writers such as Karen Armstrong produce a steady stream of bestsellers,[5] claiming ever-greater abilities to understand Muslims and thereby to get alongside them.

But is understanding without the answering of apologetics feasible or, indeed, defensible? Does seeking understanding of Muslim people and leaving it at that represent a sell out? Does it involve intentionally turning a blind eye to aspects of the theological system of Islam which can be challenged and should be answered?

At the same time, is it possible to answer the challenges that Islam levels without seeking to understand Muslim people? Does such an apologetics approach sometimes involve Christianising Islam to the point where the faith is unrecognisable to its followers? Is answering without understanding a kind of bubble that gives apologists a sense of security but has little impact on meaningful Christian-Muslim engagement?

To address these questions, we will focus on a particular set of literary materials: commentaries on the Qur'an, a field known in English by the term quranic exegesis and in Arabic as *tafsir al-Qur'an*. I have spent a significant part of my scholarly career engaged in the study of *tafsir*, which is the term I will use in this paper. That has involved surveying a wide range of Arabic commentaries dating back to the 8th century, as well as a number of commentaries in Malay/Indonesian that have drawn significantly on the earlier Arabic source commentaries. It is a field that is demanding intellectually and, therefore, satisfying. However, it is also potentially esoteric and detached from reality. To avoid that pitfall, students of *tafsir* need to keep asking themselves the question "So what?"

In this paper we will first undertake a brief survey of the Qur'an and key works of *tafsir*. We will extract from the *tafsir* materials a number of key comments by Muslim exegetes that

---

[4] Cf the Prince Alwaleed bin Talal Center for Muslim-Christian Understanding at Georgetown University, USA.

[5] Cf Armstrong's bestseller *Islam: A Short History*, The Modern Library, New York, 2002.

demonstrate why understanding *tafsir* is not enough; it must be answered as well.

The Qur'an and its exegesis

The Qur'an is roughly the same size as the New Testament. It consists of around 6,200 verses, divided into 114 chapters or *suras*, with each chapter identified according to whether it comes from Muhammad's years in Mecca or Medina.

The chapters of the Qur'an are not arranged chronologically; indeed, they are roughly arranged according to length, beginning with longer chapters and ending with shorter ones. By contrast, the books of the Bible roughly follow a chronological order. If the books of the Bible were arranged along the lines of the chapters of the Qur'an, the result would resemble the following:

Books	Verses	Books	Verses
Psalms	2526	*Rev*	404
Genesis	1533	*Heb*	303
Jeremiah	1364	Ezra	280
Isaiah	1291	Esther	272
Numbers	1289	*2 Cor*	256
Ezekiel	1271	Ecclesiastes	222
Exodus	1213	Zechariah	211
Luke	1151	Hosea	197
Matt	1071	*Eph*	155
Job	1068	Lamentations	154
Acts	1006	*Gal*	149
Deuteronomy	959	Amos	146
1 Chronicles	943	Song of Solomon	117
Proverbs	915	*1 Tim*	113
John	879	*James*	108
Leviticus	859	Micah	105
2 Chronicles	821	*1 Peter*	105
1 Kings	817	*1 John*	105
1 Samuel	810	*Phil*	104
2 Kings	719	*Col*	95
2 Samuel	695	*1Thess*	89
Mark	678	Ruth	85
Joshua	658	*2 Tim*	83
Judges	618	Joel	73
Daniel	530	*2 Peter*	61
1 Cor	437	Habakkuk	56
Rom	433	Malachi	55
Nehemiah	405	Zephaniah	53
		Jonah	48
		Nahum	47
		2Thess	47
		Titus	46
		Haggai	38
		Phlm	25
		Jude	25
		Obadiah	21
		3 John	15
		2 John	13

Were the Bible to be arranged according to the above table, two key elements that would be lost would be the sense of progressive revelation that is so key to Biblical understanding, as well as a grasp of the crucial biblical account of salvation history. Another result would be a greater tendency to proof-text in quoting the Bible; indeed, this is a common feature where the non-chronological Qur'an is cited.[6]

However, even when a reader of the Qur'an has been through a process of studying the text, it is not enough to simply stop there, because the Qur'an, like any sacred text claiming to contain divine wisdom, does not exist within a vacuum. The Qur'an is surrounded by a vast body of literature of various styles and genres which explain the text in various and, at times, contradictory ways. This gets to the very heart of the task facing the student of *tafsir*: how to read the Qur'an while looking sideways at its surrounding literature and making sense of it all.

We will now take several steps on our journey towards understanding and answering. First, we will read a segment of Qur'anic text in English translation. We will consider how various translations add extra information. We will then turn our attention to the works of *tafsir*, to see how they in turn add information to the core Qur'anic message. Having thus achieved a certain level of understanding, we will then proceed to answer the challenges that emerge from our study of the Qur'an and its commentaries.

Reading the text: *Sura al-Fatiha*
The very first chapter of the Qur'an is, for many Muslims, the most important chapter because it provides a central part of the daily prayer ritual. While many Muslims cannot recite any other part of the Qur'an, most can recite this short chapter of seven verses. We will therefore focus our study on what is an essential element of both Islam's text and the lived reality of the worldwide Muslim community.

---

[6] For a fuller discussion of this, cf. P. Riddell, "Reading the Qur'ān Chronologically: An Aid to Discourse Coherence and Thematic Development", in M. Daneshgar & W. Saleh (eds), *Islamic Studies Today: Essays in Honor of Andrew Rippin*, Leiden: Brill, 2016, 297-316.

A modern translation of this chapter reads as follows:[7]

1. *In the name of God, the Lord of Mercy, the Giver of Mercy!*
2. *Praise belongs to God, Lord of the Worlds,*
3. *the Lord of Mercy, the Giver of Mercy,*
4. *Master of the Day of Judgement.*
5. *It is You we worship; it is You we ask for help.*
6. *Guide us to the straight path:*
7. *the path of those You have blessed, those who incur no anger and who have not gone astray.*

It is not enough to simply read a translated text such as the above and to assume that the message of the chapter has been fully grasped. To illustrate this, we presented below an alternative translation:[8]

1. In the Name of Allah, the Most Beneficent, the Most Merciful.	1. In the Name of Allah, the Most Beneficent, the Most Merciful.
2. All the praises and thanks be to Allah, the Lord of the 'Alamin.	2. All the praises and thanks be to Allah, the Lord of the 'Alamin (mankind, jinns and all that exists).
3. The Most Beneficent, the Most Merciful.	3. The Most Beneficent, the Most Merciful.
4. The Only Owner of the Day of Recompense	4. The Only Owner (and the Only Ruling Judge) of the Day of Recompense (i.e. the Day of Resurrection)
5. You we worship, and You we ask for help	5. You (Alone) we worship, and You (Alone) we ask for help (for each and everything).
6. Guide us to the Straight Way	6. Guide us to the Straight Way
7. The Way of those on whom You have bestowed Your Grace, not of those who earned Your Anger, nor of those who went astray.	7. The Way of those on whom You have bestowed Your Grace, not (the way) of those who earned Your Anger (such as the Jews), nor of those who went astray (such as the Christians).

---

[7] Abdel Haleem, *The Qur'an. A new translation*, Oxford, 2004.

[8] M.T. Al-Hilali & M.M. Khan, *The Noble Qur'an*, Dar-us-Salam, 1999.

The text in the right box above presents the full translation of *Sura* 1 as presented by Al-Hilali and Khan. In the text in the left box we have stripped away the exegetical additions added within parentheses. These additions alone highlight the potential for expanded meaning within the quranic text.

What have we learnt from the brief exegetical additions provided in parentheses in the translation by Al-Hilali and Khan? First, Abdel Haleem's "Lord of the Worlds" (v2) is helpfully explained by Al-Hilali and Khan to encompass humankind, the spiritual realm and all of creation. Second, the term "Master" provided by Abdel Haleem (v4) is expanded by Al-Hilali and Khan to become "the Only Ruling Judge". Third, in translating verse 5, Al-Hilali and Khan are much more emphatic in stressing that God **alone** is to be worshipped, without associates. This addition paves the way for verse 7.

In the final verse, Abdel Haleem indicates by his translation that God is gracious towards some people, while others have earned his anger, and yet others have gone astray. However, the translator does not link these three groups with particular communities of faith.

In contrast, Al-Hilali and Khan specify that it is Jews who earn God's anger, and it is Christians who have gone astray. The reader senses that this specification of Jews and Christians in verse 7 is linked with verse 5, where Al-Hilali and Khan stress that only God should be worshipped, none other.

So, a simple reading of the text of one small chapter of the Qur'an, with a comparison of the different translations, has greatly assisted us on the path to understanding. But it has also raised certain issues that may require an answer. However, before we proceed to that point, we will expand our understanding with reference to the *tafsir* materials.

Adding the commentaries

Christian and Jewish readers of Al-Hilali and Khan's translation of Q1:7 have grounds for concern that this translation indicates to Muslim readers that God is angry with Jews and

70

considers Christians to have gone astray. Where do Al-Hilali and Khan get this information from?

A logical first point of reference in associated literature is the second source of Islamic sacred text: the Hadith. These materials are considered as records of Muhammad statements and deeds, so they carry a lot of weight and credibility. Are the Hadith materials able to shed light on the troublesome 7th verse of Qur'an chapter 1? In fact, there is a Hadith account found in two of the authoritative Sunni collections of Hadith: those by Al-Tirmidhi and Abu Dawud. It reads as follows:[9]

> Narrated Abi ibn Hatim: I asked Allah's Messenger about the Statement of Allah: "Gharil maghdubi 'alaihim [not (the way) of those who earned Your Anger],"[10] he replied: "They are the Jews". And: "Wa la d dallin (nor of those who went astray)," he replied: "The Christians, and they are the ones who went astray".

So, on our first check of materials beyond the Qur'an itself, it appears that Al-Hilali and Khan are on solid ground in their interpretation of Q1:7. What do the established commentaries have to say?

We will first consider the famous Jalalayn commentary. It was written by a teacher-student duo, Jalal al-Din al-Mahalli (d. 1459) and Jalal al-Din al-Suyuti (d. 1505). Although it largely dates from the 15th century, it continues to exert a vast influence in the world of Islam and is arguably the most widely distributed commentary on the Qur'an, both in the Arab world and beyond, throughout Islamic history. How does it interpret Q1:7?[11]

> [1:7] the path of those whom You have favoured, with guidance ... not [the path] of those against whom there is wrath, namely, the Jews, and nor of those who are astray, namely, the Christians. The subtle meaning implied by this substitution is that the guided ones are neither the Jews nor the Christians. But God knows best what is right, and to Him is the Return and the [final] Resort...

---

[9] Sam Shamoun, "Praying Not to Be Jewish or Christian", http://www.answering-islam.org/authors/shamoun/pray_not_to_be_christian.html, accessed January 25, 2018

[10] i.e. Q1:7.

[11] Jalal al-Din al-Mahalli & Jalal al-Din al-Suyuti, *Tafsir al-Jalalayn*, trans. F. Hamza, Amman: Royal Aal al-Bayt Institute for Islamic Thought, 2007, 1.

Although once again Jews and Christians are identified as the negative referents in Q1:7, a little relief is provided by the final sentence: "God knows best". However, such a nuanced final sentence would be lost on many Muslim readers of this commentary.

In engaging with the world of *tafsir*, it is important to trawl widely, considering both classical and modern, non-Sufi and Sufi, Sunni and Shi'a, and Arab and non-Arab works. In this paper we do not have the room to consider all the possibilities, but we will include a limited variety of works.

How does a modern Shi'ite commentator interpret Q1:7? To answer this we will turn to Muhammad Husayn Tabataba'i (1903–81) and his massive commentary *Tafsir al-Mizan*. This work's commentary on the seven verses of *Sura al-Fatiha* occupies 14,518 words! However, verse 7 is NOT associated with Jews and Christians in this work, but rather references to those with whom God is angry and who have gone astray are taken to point to polytheism and injustice. Tabataba'i takes a refreshingly inclusivist approach in stating:[12]

> *All divine religions are, thus, the same and the fundamental truths are common to all. The previous people have preceded us in this path. Therefore, Allah has ordered us to look into their affairs, to take lessons from them and to follow them to spiritual perfection.*

So, Christians and Jews are off the hook … for the moment. Let us cast the net more widely and consider a Sufi interpretation, drawing on the commentary by the famous Andalusian icon of monistic Sufism, Ibn al-Arabi (d. 1240). He has the following to say about Q1:7:[13]

> *[1:7] not [the path] of those against whom there is wrath, those who stop at the outward [aspects], … [stopping] short of the spiritual realities and the bliss of the heart and the tasting through the intellect, such as the Jews… nor of those who are astray, those who stand [content] with the inner aspects … They are unmindful of the manifest nature of the Truth … and have thus been denied the*

---

[12] Allamah Sayyid Muhammad Husayn at-Tabataba'i, Al-mizan an Exegesis of the Qur'an, Volume 1, Lulu Press, 2014.

[13] http://www.altafsir.com/Books/kashani.pdf, page 8, accessed January 25, 2018.

witnessing of the beauty of the Beloved in all things, as is the case with the Christians.

As with the Jalalayn commentary above, Ibn al-Arabi identifies both Jews and Christians by name as earning God's wrath and being astray respectively. However, he adds a very interesting twist in the form of a very Sufi interpretation. God is wrathful with the Jews because they are preoccupied by outward legalism and do not sufficiently acknowledge "the spiritual realities". At the same time, Christians have gone astray because they are overly preoccupied with "the inner aspects".

Moving further east, we will also consider a *tafsir* work from Islamic Southeast Asia, the multi-volume *Tafsir An Nur* by T.M. Hasbi Ash Shiddieqy (1904–75). The following translated excerpt of his commentary on Q1:7 is pertinent to our discussion:

> *The meaning of al-maghdubi 'alayhim = "Those who are rebuked", is: those who have been given the true religion that Allah has prescribed for his servants, but they refuse and turn their backs on it. ... And the meaning of wa la al-dalin = "and not those who are astray", is: all those who do not know the truth or do not yet know it correctly. A revelation or calls to faith have either not reached such groups at all, or only vaguely.*

Ash Shiddieqy unpacks his thinking further but does not link the two groups with Jews and Christians overtly at any point.

So, on the basis of the investigation so far, two out of four commentaries have given Jews and Christians bad press in interpreting Q1:7. How representative of the *tafsir* materials is this outcome? In the following table, we summarise the findings from consulting eight further prominent commentaries on the Qur'an, drawing on classical and modern, Sunni and Shi'a, and Arab and non-Arab materials.

We have consulted 12 prominent commentaries on the Qur'an, from different periods and various sectarian streams and regions. Of the 12, six have identified Jews and Christians by name with Q1:7, as earning God's wrath and being astray. The other six have translated that verse in question without making overt reference to Jews and Christians.

Identifies Q1:7 with Jews and Christians?	YES	NO
Muqatil ibn Sulayman (d. 723)	☑	
Abū Jaʿfar Muḥammad al-Tabari (d. 923)	☑	
Abu al-Qasim Mahmud al-Zamakhshari (d. 1144)	☑	
Nizam al-Din Al-Nisaburi (d. 1328/9) [blessed =; wrath = people of negligence; astray = people of immoderation]		☒
Ismail ibn Kathir (d. 1373)	☑	
Muhammad Murtada al-Kashi (d. 1505) [blessed = party of Ali; wrath = enemies of Ali; astray = doubters]		☒
Abu'l A'la Mawdudi (d. 1979) [Translates in same way as Abdel Haleem]		☒
Sayyid Qutb (d. 1966) [blessed = followers of the straight path; wrath = deviators; astray = heedless]		☒

Before we turn to the question of answering the challenge, a further thought arises. Do those six commentaries which do not overtly mention Jews and Christians absolve these faith communities of all responsibility for the excesses referred to in Q1:7? Let us look more closely at the commentary by the Indonesian scholar T.M. Hasbi Ash Shiddieqy. His full comment on Q1:7 reads as follows, translated from the Indonesian original:[14]

> *The meaning of al-maghdubi 'alayhim = "Those who are rebuked", is: those who have been given the true religion that Allah has prescribed for his servants, but they refuse and turn their backs on it. They are not willing to pay attention to the signs that are presented to them because of their uncritical following [of their existing beliefs]. They blindly follow superseded leftovers of their forebears. They face dire consequences; immersion in the fires of hell.*
>
> *And the meaning of wa la al-dalin = "and not those who are astray", is: all those who do not know the truth or do not yet know it correctly. A revelation or calls to faith have either not reached such groups at all, or only vaguely. Therefore, they are confused and in error, lacking corrective guidance. This group, if not misguided in matters of the world, are perverted in the affairs of the*

---

[14] T.M. Hasbi Ash Shiddieqy, *Tafsir Al Quranul Madjied An-Nur*, Jakarta: Bulan Bintang, 1965, vol. 1, 46–47.

Hereafter. People who are not given religion appear to be in states of chaos in all aspects of living.

In this case, this group is not weighed down by observing the Shari'a and by [seeking to avoid] punishment in the Hereafter.

This is the view of most religious scholars.

A group of scholars are of the opinion that an individual's own reason is sufficient to meet religious requirements. So the person who has the gift of reason, bears the responsibility of heeding the heavens and the earth and paying close attention to the events of nature, and his obligations towards the Creator, although only being able to call on the fruit of his intellect and the result of his reasoning. In this way, he is released from the punishment of Hell on the Day of Resurrection. Otherwise, he will certainly perish as well.

Two key observations can be helpfully drawn from this commentary. First, those guilty of either turning their back on the revelation given to them or being "perverted in the affairs of the Hereafter" face dire consequences: Hell fire. Readers are left in no doubt as to the fate of such people. The likelihood is that any readers who read other commentaries which do identify Jews and Christians with this verse would in all likelihood carry over that association when reading this commentary by Ash Shiddieqy. In other words, this commentary has considerable potential for reinforcing the overt critique of Jews and Christians found in other works of exegesis.

A secondary observation relates to the interesting final paragraph of the quotation. It allows for a kind of natural theology, where those who do not embrace the religion of truth can nevertheless glean sufficient amounts of divine truth from the natural order. So, on this score as well, Jews and Christians seem to have no excuse for not embracing Islam.

Answering the challenge

How important is this issue for Christian-Muslim relations? We need to recall that *Sura al-Fatiha* is recited in each of the daily prayers. Admittedly, the exegetical addition naming Jews and Christians does not form part of that daily recitation. Nevertheless, as Muslims learn the text from their religious leaders and receive associated explanations of meaning, the likelihood is significant that vast numbers of Muslims are reminded on a daily basis of negative perceptions of the Jews and Christians. This is the stuff of which hostile stereotypes and religious slurs are made.

Mark Durie articulates the challenge well in writing:[15]

To be genuine and effective, reconciliation between Muslims and those they refer to as 'People of the Book' (Jews and Christians), requires that Al-Fatihah and its meaning be discussed openly. That devout Muslims are daily declaring before Allah that Christians have gone astray and Jews are objects of divine wrath, must be considered a matter of central importance for interfaith relations. This is all the more so because the interpretation of verse 7 which relates it to Christians and Jews is soundly based upon the words of Muhammad himself. As Al-Fatihah is the daily worship of Muslims, and represents the very essence of Islam itself, the meaning of these words cannot be ignored or glossed over.

This brings us back to our discussion at the beginning. We have expended considerable energy in seeking to understand the particular issue at hand: interpretation within the world of Islam of *Sura al-Fatiha*, especially verse seven. It has raised issues of concern. Therefore is it sufficient to simply understand or are answers required?

Clearly, answers are required if Christians are to cement good relationships with Muslims and to prevent the exegesis of Q1:7 from poisoning Christian-Muslim relations. We offer below a set of activities that both answer the challenge posed by Q1:7 and potentially contribute to better Christian-Muslim relationships. Christians should assess each suggestion to determine the best match for individual personalities and gifts. Christians should also give thought to additional activities, as the following list is intended to begin a process, rather than be all-encompassing.

So how should Christians respond?
1. Ask your Muslim friends about this famous *Sura* of the Qur'an, using the conversation to introduce the Lord's Prayer.
2. Prepare a group from your church to dialogue with Muslims on The Lord's Prayer and *Sura al-Fatiha*.
3. Ask your early questions about the easier issues arising from *Sura al-Fatiha*.

---

[15] http://blog.markdurie.com/2009/12/greatest-recitation-of-surat-al-fatiha.html cited 1 April, 2017

     a. Lord of the *'Alamin* (mankind, jinns and all that exists).

     b. The Only Owner (and the Only Ruling Judge) of the Day of Recompense (i.e. the Day of Resurrection).

     c. NB Listen with interest but also ensure you contribute Christian perspectives and scripture.

4. Engage in online dialogue with Muslims (dozens of websites) about *Sura al-Fatiha* and its interpretation.

5. After building a relationship and covering easier topics in dialogue (individual, group, online), bring up the matter of Allah being wrathful with Jews and considering Christians to have gone astray.

6. Study more about Islam, to understand and to answer.

Further reading

Gatje, Helmut. *The Qur'an and its Exegesis*, Rockport, Maine: Oneworld Publications, c1996

Mawdudi, M. Abu al-A'la d. 1979. *The Meaning of the Qur'an Tafhim al-Qur'an.* Composed in Urdu and translated into Arabic and English Lahore, 1967-, http://www.englishtafsir.com/

Qutb, Sayyid, *In the Shade of the Qur'an*, https://www.kalamullah.com/shade-of-the-quran.html

Tafsir Ibn Kathir, http://www.qtafsir.com/

Von Denffer, A. *Ulum al-Qur'an*, Leicester: Islamic Foundation, 1994, http://majalla.org/books/2004/intro-to-quran/1-intoduction-to-the-quran.pdf   ; http://www.islamicbulletin.org/free_downloads/quran/u l_umal_quran.pdf

Various translations into English of leading Arabic commentaries on the Qur'an uploaded at http://altafsir.com/

UNDERSTANDING AND ANSWERING ISLAM
What now?

Dan Paterson

1 Corinthians 9:19-23

> *For though I am free from all, I have made myself a servant to all, that I might win more of them. To the Jews I became as a Jew, in order to win Jews. To those under the law I became as one under the law (though not being myself under the law) that I might win those under the law. To those outside the law I became as one outside the law (not being outside the law of God but under the law of Christ) that I might win those outside the law. To the weak I became weak, that I might win the weak. I have become all things to all people, that by all means I might save some. I do it all for the sake of the gospel, that I may share with them in its blessings.*[1]

A New Vision for Humanity

What is it that makes the final vision of Scripture, that of the New Heavens and the New Earth, so unique and attractive? What does it say, is the *telos* (end, purpose goal) of all of human history and hope? Notice a few things. Revelation 21 paints a picture where Heaven and Earth collapse into one another as God's space and human space become one. We're also told that people of every tribe and tongue and nation and culture are gathered together into a new humanity. Even the geography changes as John envisions a world where there is no *sea*. Why? Because to him, an elderly man exiled on an island, a body of water is what stood

---

[1] English Standard Version (ESV) The Holy Bible, English Standard Version. ESV® Text Edition: 2016. Copyright © 2001 by Crossway Bibles, a publishing ministry of Good News Publishers.

between him and those he loved. Barriers are broken down or bridged as the "kings of the earth" bring their splendour into the New Jerusalem. The best products of every human culture, having passed through the fires of judgment, are now brought together in worship to God. And surely it is something of this vision that informs the Apostle Paul as he writes here: that he shares *with them* in the blessings of the gospel.

I stand in a strange place. Amongst those presenting at this conference I'm the least qualified to speak. My everyday routines rarely bring me into contact with practising Muslims. But I'm not untouched by a love for Muslims. One of my closest friends in High School fled Iraq with his parents under the regime of Suddam Hussein. As Shi'ite Muslims they faced serious threats. My friend went on after school to study dentistry, and I became a Christian. We lost touch for years until through the wonders of Facebook, we reconnected, only to discover he has returned to the Middle East, now in the UAE, and is pursuing theological study in Islam. Now, away from his multicultural experience of High School, and thrust into deep Islamic community, I wonder what may have been different if I had heeded Paul's clarion call and taken responsibility to *win* him. For that's what love does.

A Deep Motivation for Apologetics
Most people aren't driven to apologetics for apologetics' sake. In my travels I find a few who are. They want to debate finer points of theistic arguments *ad nauseam*. But that is not how most of us are wired. I got into apologetics because at a crucial time, when I was asking big questions about meaning, purpose and suffering in life, I encountered the claims of Jesus of Nazareth and I found that they made more sense of my question than anything else. Then, when I went on to try and share my faith in Jesus it seemed everyone had their own set of questions and barriers that had to be addressed as part of the conversation.

Love dictates that if I care about someone enough then I take them and their questions seriously. I should understand their story and be aware of how they think. I should care about their categories and the desires that drive them. If I want them to encounter the Christ whom I worship, then I need to speak to both their mind and their heart. As the messenger, although the message isn't flexible and cannot be changed, I must be. Why? Because God didn't just send another book from Heaven rather He put on flesh to be like us and amongst us. God became as a Jew to reach the Jews and in the same way the Apostle Paul became as a Greek or as a Roman to reach those around him.

Prepared to give an answer
Over the course of this weekend conference a few things have stood out through the talks from our speakers that I hope will come to shape us as we move forward in our ministry.

We need to be driven by love to see Muslims won to Jesus
Paul longed to see the people of the book bend the knee to their Messiah. He would have traded his own salvation if he could that they might worship Jesus. And here we need to ask ourselves a question: *do we have this same love within us?*

If this love is lacking for our Muslim neighbours — our friends, the refugees that are coming to our shores, the international students that are coming to our universities, our Uber drivers — then this whole endeavour must start by us being driven to our knees.

> PRAYER: *Holy Father, break our hearts for those trapped in Islam with the dim and distorted light that it sheds on who you are. Allow us to see them not according to our world's suspicious eyes but according to your immeasurable love.*

We need to train so that we are ready to engage
Only this kind of love will motivate us to spend enough time engaging with the content from our speakers so as to make it our own; to train ourselves so that it is *useful*. After speaking of becoming all things to all people, the Apostle Paul picks up on athletic metaphors to describe the need for training to achieve our desired goals. Not long ago, teaching on this passage, I interviewed one of a few Olympic gold medallist swimmers at our church. When I asked how hard she trained to compete at that level, her answer challenged the audience. Every week she had 8 swim sessions for conditioning and technique and 3 gym sessions for muscle strengthening. But outside of the pool and gym hours, her pursuit consumed her life. It dictated what she ate, how much she slept, what social situations she entered. She shaped her whole life around reaching that goal by entering *strict training*. And if she does this for a perishable crown (or in her case a gold medal), how much

more should we train to help our Muslim neighbours be won to Christ?

This is why when the Apostle Paul went to the Jews he reasoned from their Scriptures, and when he went to the Greeks, he built upon their poets and philosophers. He *studied* and knew his stuff so as to be *useful* in reaching those to whom he was sent. And when you study the verbs in the book of Acts that describe how the first followers of Jesus went about sharing the gospel, it wasn't a dispassionate presentation. Of the 26 verbs that describe their ministry, 17 carry strong notions of *persuasion*. They were reasoning, refuting, debating, arguing, testifying, disputing, speaking true and rational words, and trying to convince. They knew what they believed and they knew why they believed it, and they would draw from these resources in making their case for Christ.

Simply put: *we need to know our stuff!* It may begin with books, or more conferences, or short–term cultural or exposure missions, or learning Arabic, or inviting our neighbours over for a meal and asking questions. You need to learn what they believe and why they believe it. There is simply no shortcut here. In the same way you don't become an Olympic athlete overnight, you're not going to instantly transform into a seasoned apologist to Muslims. But start somewhere.

When I was studying in England I had two encounters in ministry to Muslims that really opened my eyes to how being ready can make a difference. The first was on the campus of York University. I was witnessing there with a dear friend from Egypt who grew up in an evangelical family. We had been learning for months from our teachers how evangelism undergirded by apologetics must always be done with gentleness and respect. I didn't realise how tremendously British my interpretation of those words had become. On one of our days there witnessing to students, my Egyptian friend was engaged in conversation with a Pakistani Muslim. Their exchange quickly became heated and drew a lot of attention as the English students didn't know whether to crowd and watch or run and hide. And after 10 minutes, the shouting match came to an end with the following exchange:

Pakistani Muslim: *"You are stupid. You should read the Koran and become a Muslim"*

Egyptian Friend: "*No, you are stupid. You should read the gospels and become a Christian.*"

I thought my friend had blown it! That he'd simply forgotten everything we had been learning. But to my surprise, the Pakistani Muslim embraced him, said he was a good man, and thanked him for being a Christian of conviction – someone who really believed it. You see my friend was experienced enough to know that *conviction is measured in tone* to many in the Middle East.

Another story comes from one of my fellow students who was a Muslim convert to Christianity. To honour her request for anonymity, I'll keep the details of this story to a minimum. Needless to say, her conversion to Christ came at great personal cost. One day in class we were asked by a professor about any evangelistic conversations we were having with people. Originally, when her turn came up, she deflected, trying not to answer. But when pushed, she shared that she was currently doing 30 individual Bible studies with Muslims in Oxford. 30! On top of a gruelling study programme and ministry requirements, she spent her late nights and early mornings introducing Muslims to Jesus through the gospel of Luke. It was in her shadow that I seriously began to question my own Christianity. Whenever we would go for a meal, you could never pay. She would always grab the bill from everyone, and when the cashier would ask why she did this, she'd always say: "*Jesus paid with his blood for me, so it's nothing for me to give what I have for others.*" And in these situations, she was always prepared. Her bag was like a prop from Mary Poppins, as though an entire other universe fit inside. For at any moment, for any situation, she would always pull out a resource (book, Bible, tract, DVD) to suit the occasion. Such an easy thing: have a book or resource ready. And yet so rarely am I prepared for that moment. I cannot tell you how many thousands will share in the blessings of the gospel from her willingness and preparedness to give.

We need to offer more than just answers

I have a number of dear friends who are same-sex attracted and have come to Christ. A couple of years ago, after being in a wedding party with one of these friends, we had a late night conversation in Atlanta, Georgia. We spoke about what it meant for him to become a Christian, and he spoke with deep feeling about the cost of giving up a tight-knit community and way of making sense of who he was to answer Christ's call. And he spoke there of the profound sense of sacrifice in laying down his right to have a romantic relationship in this life, wondering then whether he was doomed to a life of loneliness. What did Christ mean when he said to his closest disciples:

> *Truly, I say to you, there is no one who has left house or brothers or sisters or mother or father or children or lands, for my sake and for the gospel, who will not receive a hundredfold now in this time, houses and brothers and sisters and mothers and children and lands, with persecutions, and in the age to come eternal life* (Mark 10:29-30.)

When we ask our Muslim neighbours, or our LGBT friends, to come follow Jesus, often by extension we're asking them to bring a sword between them and their closest relationships. Allegiance to Jesus means every other identity marker takes a back seat or must be respectfully left behind, which sadly often leads to being ostracised from loved ones or from a community that served as their family. What then does Christ demand of us? To wish them well in the Lord and connect them to a Church? Heaven forbid.

Jesus said that it is the love of the Christian community that will be our true identity marker as followers of Jesus (John 13:35). Whatever we ask our Muslim friends to sacrifice is precisely what Jesus intends us to become to them. Will your home become their home? Your spare room their room? Your dinner table their own? Your family their family?

Christians tend to be known to the Muslim world as apathetic sellouts. But how different would their vision be if they saw us living in obedience to the commands of Christ and putting the beauty of the gospel on display? Love will always be the greatest apologetic for Christianity and for the Church. And in 1 Peter 3 we're not asked to give an answer to everyone, but to everyone who *asks for the reason for our hope*. You see, the Apostle Peter presupposes that our lives are piquing curiosity in the eyes of our neighbours. The Christian calibre of our lives should provoke questions to which the gospel is the answer.

CONTRIBUTORS

Dr **Richard Shumack** gained his PhD from the University of Melbourne, Australia, where he examined contemporary Muslim philosophy and discovered Muslim thinking to be especially weak in their bold claims to certainty. Richard is Director of the Arthur Jeffery Centre for the Study of Islam at Melbourne School of Theology and a research fellow at the Centre for Public Christianity in Sydney, Australia. He teaches regularly on ministry in Muslim contexts in Australian seminaries, universities, churches and mission organisations. His publications include a training book *Witnessing to Western Muslims* and the philosophical apologetic *The Wisdom of Islam and the Foolishness of Christianity*.

Dr **Andy Bannister** is Director of the Solas Centre for Public Christianity and an Adjunct Speaker for Ravi Zacharias International Ministries. He has spoken in hundreds of universities, churches, business settings and on TV and radio. Andy holds a PhD in Quranic Studies and is an Adjunct Research Fellow at the Arthur Jeffery Centre for the Study of Islam at Melbourne School of Theology. He is the author of two books, *An Oral-Formulaic Study of the Qur'an* (a ground-breaking and innovative study that reveals many of the ways the Qur'an was first composed) and *The Atheist Who Didn't Exist (or: The Dreadful Consequences of Really Bad Arguments),* a humorous engagement with the New Atheism. He also co-wrote and presented the TV documentary, *Burning Questions.* When not travelling, speaking or writing, Andy is a keen hiker, mountain climber and photographer. He is married to Astrid and they have two children, Caitriona and Christopher. They live in Dundee in Scotland.

Dr **Bernie Power** holds degrees in science, arts and theology. He worked as a mission partner with Interserve for 21 years in Asia and the Middle East in Muslim-majority countries. He lectures in Islamic Studies at the Melbourne School of Theology and works with CultureConnect in Melbourne. He completed his doctorate on the Hadith and has written three books on the

Muslim-Christian interface: *Understanding Jesus and Muhammad: What the Ancient Texts say about them; Challenging Islamic Traditions: Searching Questions about the Hadith from a Christian Perspective; Engaging Islamic Traditions: Using the Hadith in Christian Ministry to Muslims.* His next book is about the Qur'an. He is married to Catherine and they have two adult sons and a grandson. His areas of academic interest include the life of Muhammad, the Qur'an, the hadith and apologetics to Islam. His aim is to help Christians understand more about Islam and for Muslims to understand more about Jesus.

Dr **Mark Durie** is an academic, human rights activist, Anglican pastor, a Shillman-Ginsburg Writing Fellow at the Middle East Forum, and Adjunct Research Fellow of the Arthur Jeffery Centre for the Study of Islam at Melbourne School of Theology. He has published many articles and books on the language and culture of the Acehnese, Christian-Muslim relations and religious freedom. He holds a PhD in Linguistics from the National University and a ThD in Quranic Theology from the Australian College of Theology. He has held visiting appointments at the University of Leiden, MIT, UCLA and Stanford, and was elected a Fellow of the Australian Academy of the Humanities in 1992.

Dr **Peter G. Riddell** is Vice Principal (Academic) at the Melbourne School of Theology and Professorial Research Associate in the Department of History at SOAS, University of London. He previously taught at the Australian National University, the Institut Pertanian Bogor (Indonesia), SOAS and the London School of Theology, where he served as Professor of Islamic Studies. He was invited as visiting professor at L'Ecole Pratique des Hautes Etudes/Sorbonne (Paris) in May/June 2015. He has published widely on the study of Southeast Asia, Islam and Christian-Muslim Relations. His books include *Transferring a Tradition* (UC Berkeley, 1990); *Islam and the Malay-Indonesian World* (London: Hurst, 2001); *Islam in Context* (with Peter Cotterell, Grand Rapids: Baker, 2003), *Christians and Muslims* (Leicester: IVP, 2004) and *Interpreting the Qur'an in 17th Century Aceh* (Leiden: Brill, 2017). He has edited over a dozen volumes, including Islam: *Essays on Scripture, Thought and Society* (with Tony Street, Leiden: Brill, 1997), *Islam and Christianity on the Edge: Talking Points in Christian-Muslim Relations into the 21st Century* (with John Azumah, Melbourne:

Acorn, 2013); and *The Qur'an in the Malay-Indonesian World: Context and Interpretation* (with Majid Daneshgar and Andrew Rippin, London: Routledge, 2016). In his spare time, he plays lead guitar and bass in worship bands.

Dan Paterson is a speaker with Ravi Zacharias International Ministries based in Brisbane, Australia. After some family tragedies in his childhood that raised a series of barriers to belief in God, Dan came to Christ at 18 through an investigation of the New Testament. Given this background, Dan developed a driving passion to study theology and apologetics to help make sense of the Christian faith to sceptics and spiritual seekers. Completing Bachelors and Masters degrees in ministry and theology, Dan pursued further training by heading with his wife to Oxford in the UK, where he completed RZIM's one-year course at the Oxford Centre for Christian Apologetics (2012/2013). Having returned to Brisbane, Dan speaks regularly to audiences across the belief spectrum on life's biggest questions. He is married to Erin, and they have two children. Dan loves reading, coffee, movies, the outdoors, and AFL.

Books Published by the Arthur Jeffery Centre for the Study of Islam[1] through the MST Press, Melbourne

Occasional Papers

Viewing Islam: From Text to Context, ed. Peter G Riddell, 2009 & 2010

Insights into Islam: Contemporary and Historical Studies on Islam and Christianity, ed. Michael Raiter, reprinted 2016

Islam and the Last Day: Christian Perspectives on Islamic Eschatology, ed. Brent Neely and Peter G Riddell, 2013-2014

Faiths in Conversation: Comparative Themes and Perspectives across the Religions, ed. Ruth Nicholls and Peter G Riddell, 2015

The Church under the Shadow of Shariah: A Christian Assessment, ed. John Cheong and Peter G. Riddell, 2016

Aubrey H. Whitehouse Series

Do you remember ...? Recollections and Reflections, Aubrey Whitehouse, Foreword, Ruth Nicholls, 2017

These books can be purchased via the Melbourne School of Theology website http://www.mst.edu.au/ajc-publications/

---

[1] The Arthur Jeffery Centre for the Study of Islam was formally known as the Centre for the Study of Islam and Other Faiths.

www.ingramcontent.com/pod-product-compliance
Lightning Source LLC
Chambersburg PA
CBHW060346050426
42336CB00050B/2109